Praise for
Bollinger on Bollinger Bands

"I'm proud to say John Bollinger has been a friend of mine for 20 years. The Wall Street community is full of very bright people, and John is one of the brightest. I have always been impressed with his intelligence, his common sense, and most of all his integrity. The Bollinger Bands he developed have become an important tool for traders looking for a simple, effective way to identify market trends. This book is a wonderful, easy-to-understand explanation of his famous baby."

BILL GRIFFETH
CNBC TV Anchor

"Get the word from the Master! Bollinger, who skillfully writes an insightful weekly commentary, has turned his skills to the trading techniques you can use to successfully trade the indicator which bears his name. The three trading schemes cover everything but range trading, and the indicator discussion is heaven for tech junkies."

JOHN SWEENEY
Editor
Technical Analysis of Stocks & Commodities

"Bollinger Bands have always been both popular and powerful. Now John explains the Bands in detail, from the Squeeze to the Walk to the relationship between the Bands and other indicators."

STEVE ACHELIS
Author of *Technical Analysis from A to Z*

BOLLINGER ON BOLLINGER BANDS

BOLLINGER ON BOLLINGER BANDS

John Bollinger, CFA, CMT

McGraw-Hill
New York Chicago San Francisco
Lisbon London Madrid Mexico City
Milan New Delhi San Juan Seoul
Singapore Sydney Toronto

Library of Congress Cataloging-in-Publication Data
Bollinger, John.
   Bollinger on Bollinger bands / by John Bollinger.
      p. cm.
   ISBN 0-07-137368-3
   1. Trading bands (Securities)   2. Investment analysis.   3. Stock price forecasting.
 4. Securities—Prices—Charts, diagrams, etc.   I. Title.

HG4529.B65   2001
332.63'222—dc21   2001030666

McGraw-Hill

A Division of The McGraw-Hill Companies

1 2 3 4 5 6 7 8 9 0   DOC/DOC   0 9 8 7 6 5 4 3 2 1

ISBN 0-07-137368-3

This book was set in Palatino by Keyword Publishing Services.

Printed and bound by R. R. Donnelley & Sons Company

This publication is designed to provide accurate and authoritative
information in regard to the subject matter covered. It is sold with the
understanding that neither the author nor the publisher is engaged in
rendering legal, accounting, futures/securities trading, or other professional
service. If legal advice or other expert assistance is required, the services of a
competent professional person should be sought.

—From a Declaration of Principles jointly adopted by a Committee
of the American Bar Association and a Committee of Publishers

 This book is printed on recycled, acid-free paper containing a
minimum of 50% recycled, de-inked fiber.

CONTENTS

LIST OF ILLUSTRATIONS

LIST OF TABLES

FOREWORD

In June of 1984 I first walked through the door of 2525 Ocean Park Boulevard in Santa Monica, California. It was the home of the Financial News Network, the nation's first television network dedicated solely to the coverage of economic, market, and business news. FNN's headquarters was an ungodly place, a ramshackle box of a two-story building. It was singularly unimpressive. Square, somewhat dilapidated, and cramped, it housed scores of employees who were charged with putting on 12 hours of business news every day, for little money and for virtually no viewers. Such was the environment I encountered exactly 17 years ago.

I took an entry-level job at FNN because neither Mr. Spielberg nor Mr. Lucas recognized my budding talent as a filmmaker. Not that they knew I existed, but while I was convinced of my potential as a world-class auteur, no one else seemed to notice my graduation from film school. Only an old friend from high school offered me gainful employment, and it was in an area of the media with which I was thoroughly unfamiliar. For me FNN was a temporary resting place, a ground-floor opportunity that would pay the bills while I peddled my scripts for mainstream TV shows and feature films that would one day soon make me rich and famous.

So I began my job at FNN with some reservation. While it represented a learning experience that could help me hone my media skills, the content was frighteningly dull, or at least I thought at the time. There were many numbers (which I did not have the head for), a lot of jargon, and there were many items I had simply never heard of ... wool futures and palm oil markets immediately leap to mind. But the people in the newsroom of

FNN were interested in all of it, which intrigued me greatly. What was it about this seemingly meaningless stuff that had an entire room full of people so fully engaged? Why were they looking at charts and graphs? What, on earth, were they talking about day in and day out? I began to get curious.

Before I expand on my growing curiosity, let me describe the working environment at Financial News Network. There were three main rooms on the first floor of the boxlike building. The newsroom, such as it was, was a 30 by 50 square with a ring of desks around the inside, outfitted with the requisite IBM Selectrics, boxes of script-sets for typing news stories and the stereotypical overflowing wastepaper baskets underneath. The writers and producers were generally quite young, in their 20s and early 30s. The senior producers were mostly older men, who had spent many years in the news business . . . a collection of hard-boiled types from print and broadcast journalists who tried, many times in vain, to give shape to this emerging brand of news reporting that had never been attempted before.

Two rooms attached to the main newsroom. One was for the associate producers and segment producers who put together the taped pieces that filled out the day's newscasts. Still another room housed some of FNN's on-air specialists, of whom John Bollinger was one. John, along with the late Ed Hart, provided much of FNN's commentary about the day's market events. Ed Hart was a grizzled veteran of business news. While working for FNN, Ed also delivered daily business reports for KFWB, a Los Angeles–area all-news radio station that battled to compete with its bigger local rival, KNX.

Ed was a curmudgeon's curmudgeon. A salty character with a taste for dirty jokes, Ed was, and shall ever remain, the best business journalist I have worked with. He had an encyclopedic knowledge of economic and market history. He had a frightening photographic memory and a rapier wit. He suffered no fools and never felt shy about identifying your intellectual shortcomings. But, he had a great heart and loved nothing more than business news, except sailing and dancing.

On one particularly busy news day, our then-managing editor walked into the newsroom while the entire staff was on deadline and asked for help with a word game with which he was struggling. Everyone else was struggling with getting a show on the air, but our fearless leader failed to notice, preoccupied with the weighty matter of completing the "jumble" or some such thing. He asked out loud if anyone knew the definition of "jejune." Only Ed Hart bothered to reply. "It's the month before Ju-July," Ed snapped, and walked away. Ed had more important things on his mind most often, and they frequently centered on being accurate, timely, and insightful. He was all of the above. He was early with his market calls, always right, and his information was delivered in a highbrow manner that will likely never be duplicated again.

FNN's other specialist sat virtually isolated in a room off to the side of the newsroom. That was John Bollinger. He was FNN's resident market technician. It was John's job to pour over charts and graphs, looking for repetitive patterns in market action and explain to FNN's audience that by identifying past patterns one could make intelligent bets on the future of the market. Stock quote machines, some primitive computers, and reams of paper surrounded John. Not to mention, all kinds of books on technical analysis, the titles of which I did not recognize at the time. Bollinger, as we called him, was a cantankerous sort of fellow, opinionated and outspoken when it came to the markets. He had quite an interesting background, which drew me to him immediately. He spent years as a cameraman, including a stint at the CBS newsmagazine *60 Minutes*. We were somewhat simpatico, since we shared a love of film and an interest in great storytelling. But I was a bit stumped why someone who had had a great job in mainstream TV would give it up to stare at squiggles on a page that presumably meant something to someone. I didn't quite get it, but as I said before, I began to get curious.

When I first arrived at FNN, I understood nothing about economics, markets, or business. But as I lingered there for a number of months, still waiting for my big box office break, I was increasingly drawn to the people and the content that defined FNN. Bill Griffeth and Sue Herera (then McMahon) were in the process of inventing business television, as we know it today. Ed Hart, John Bollinger, and a senior producer, one Doug Crichton, would hold fascinating conversations about current events, business, markets, and economics that I did not pretend to understand. But they hooked me on the content. I became a business news junkie and it's an addiction that lasts to this day.

John Bollinger is one of the people who really hooked me at FNN. His enthusiasm for the subject matter was contagious. His passion for learning more and more about markets and their history was inspiring. And his attention to detail raised the performance bar for the rest of us who were constantly struggling to keep up with his insatiable appetite for information. As John grew in his knowledge of the markets, his insights became increasingly useful to those around him. We were all impressed by the speed with which he assimilated market messages and explained their meaning to our audience.

It became increasingly clear to those of us who worked with John that he would one day make important contributions to the field of technical analysis. What once was really a Wall Street backwater had grown into a very respectable form of market analysis. Great technicians like Joe Granville, Robert Farrell, Edson Gould, Robert Prechter, and, of course, Charles Dow invented forms of market analysis that survive to this day. Indeed, all of Wall Street's major brokerage houses, money management firms, and big hedge funds employ technical analysts. All investors look constantly for an edge. Technical analysis is one of the tools that can provide that edge which means the difference between profit and loss.

As I said, many of John's colleagues believed it was only a matter of time before John joined the ranks of important analysts who would change the way technical analysis was conducted and considered. And, indeed, he has.

Bollinger on Bollinger Bands is a must read for all students of the markets. It explains and expounds on an important contribution to technical analysis that John made while we were working together at the Financial News Network. When John first invented Bollinger Bands, I didn't understand the significance of his work. As I stated, it took me many years to understand fully the subject I was covering, and John's work, at the time, was as arcane as any I had encountered. (Gladly that is no longer so, lest some of you worry that I am still unfamiliar with technical analysis.)

But like many great discoveries, Bollinger Bands are elegant in their simplicity. They define the parameters that accompany market gyrations. They set the boundaries for expectations, and they allow traders to understand the degree and speed with which markets can move. Bollinger Bands bend, yet they are made to be broken. It is when they are broken that they contain some of the most important information an investor could want. They are mathematical in their construction but, in pictures, they paint a thousand words that are invaluable for investors.

In short, Bollinger Bands are a technical tool which all investors, traders, and money managers should understand and utilize. And they are only one of several contributions to market analysis that their namesake has made and for which he will be remembered well.

RON INSANA
CNBC
June 2001

PREFACE

My first encounter with the stock market came as a child in the form of a bequest of a few shares of Fruhauf, a company that subsequently took a long time to go bankrupt. My second encounter came as a young man, in the late 1960s, while working for the Museum of the Media, an institution owned by three brothers whose father was a highly successful underwriter of high-tech stocks at the time. High-tech stocks were all the rage, and my supervisor fell under the influence. Without really understanding the details, I instinctively knew something wasn't quite right. Next came the mid-1970s and an assessment of the damage done to my mother by holding mutual funds through a bear market. My final formative acquaintance came in the late 1970s when oil was "on its inevitable way to $50 or $100 barrel" and oil stocks were all the rage, especially small companies involved in deep drilling for gas in places like Oklahoma's Anadarko basin. Needless to say, oil went down instead of up, and oil stocks in general were crushed, with many of the marginal stocks disappearing altogether.

There had to be a better way, and I looked for that better way for a long time without finding it. In the end I had to create it. It is called Rational Analysis. RA is the combination of technical analysis and fundamental analysis in a relative framework (Figure P.1). This book focuses on the primary RA tool, Bollinger Bands, which provide the relative framework; a subsequent—larger—volume will focus on Rational Analysis itself.

To define terms:

Technical Analysis: The study of market-related data as an aid to investment decision making

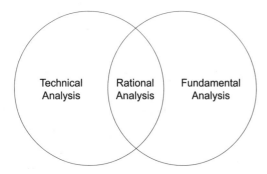

Figure P.1 Rational Analysis

> **Fundamental Analysis:** The study of company-related data as an aid to investment decision making
> **Rational Analysis:** The juncture of the sets of technical and fundamental analysis[1]

Technical analysts believe that all useful information is already impounded in the price structure. Therefore the best source of information is the price structure itself. Fundamental analysts estimate the worth of a share based on company and economic factors and compare their estimate with the market price. If there is a sufficient discrepancy, they act. In essence, technicians believe that the market is right, while fundamental analysts believe their analysis is right.

It is important to keep in mind that the stock is not the company and the company is not the stock. Though there is a relationship between a company and its stock, the connective tissue between the two is primarily psychological. Traditionally it is thought that a company's fundamentals ultimately determine the stock price. Here are a couple of counterexamples: A falling stock price can hurt a company. If key employees with stock options see the price plummet, they may go elsewhere in search of better compensation. Or even more damning, a falling stock price may prevent a company from getting the financing it needs to stay alive. No matter what the case, those investors using Rational Analysis have the upper hand, as they understand both the stock and the company.

At the end of the day it is the combination of technical and fundamental analysis that best paves the road to investment success. Employing such a combination creates an environment within which the investor or trader can make rational decisions, an environment in which emotions can be kept under control.

Emotions are the investor's worst enemy. Did you ever sell into a panic, buy at the top, worry about being caught in a bear market, or fear missing the next big bull run? Rational Analysis can help you avoid those traps by giving you a reasonable basis to make fully informed decisions. Then, instead of being a member of the crowd, swayed by greed and fear and making the same mistakes time and again, you can hold your head up high as an independent investor acting in your own best interest.

Finally, to start off on the right foot, a definition: Bollinger Bands are bands drawn in and around the price structure on a chart (see Figure P.2). Their purpose is to provide relative definitions of high and low; prices near the upper band are high,

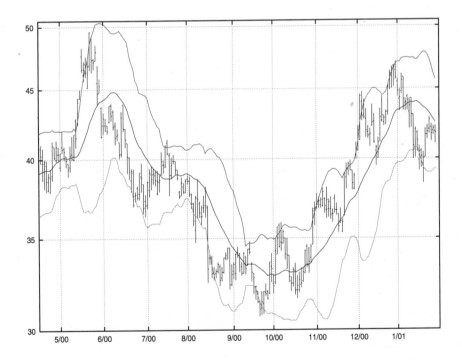

Figure P.2   Bollinger Bands, Deere & Co., 200 days.

Table P.1   Standard Bollinger Band Formulas

Upper band = Middle band + 2 standard deviations
Middle band = 20-period moving average
Lower band = Middle band − 2 standard deviations

prices near the lower band are low. The base of the bands is a moving average that is descriptive of the intermediate-term trend (see Table P.1). This average is known as the middle band and its default length is 20 periods. The width of the bands is determined by a measure of volatility called standard deviation. The data for the volatility calculation is the same data that was used for the moving average. The upper and lower bands are drawn at a default distance of two standard deviations from the average.

Now that we know what Bollinger Bands are, let's learn how to use them.

JOHN BOLLINGER

ACKNOWLEDGMENTS

We do nothing alone.

First my parents—my father, who taught me math was fun and how to fly, and my mother, who had the faith to place her future in my hands.

My wife Dorit, without whom all of this simply would not have been possible, and my daughter Zoë, upon whom the sun does not set.

Jon Ratner, a broker with AG Becker when I met him, now a valued friend, made many things possible, most importantly via an introduction to Charles Speth and Holly Hendricks at whose firm I learned about trading. Later he convinced his office manager to provide me with a quote machine and a desk from which to conduct my seminal operations.

Earl Brian, the chairman of the board of the Financial News Network, who believed both in me and in computerized technical analysis.

Marc Chaikin, Steve Leuthold, Don Worden, and Jim Yates, who taught me concepts and techniques at a time when I was hungry for them, and Arthur Merrill, who set an impossibly high standard.

The data used in the charts and testing process for this book was provided by Bridge, http://www.bridge.com, via Bridge-Station. The testing was largely done in Microsoft Excel. The charts in this book were mostly created with gnuplot, an open-source scientific plotting program. I wrote a gnuplot preprocessor in Microsoft Visual BASIC that retrieved the Bridge data via DDE, prepared the gnuplot scripts, and wrote data files for the charts.

Open-source software is the cutting edge of the computer world, and I am deeply indebted to the many fine programmers who so selflessly contribute their fine work to operating systems such as Linux and programs such as gnuplot. To find out more about gnuplot, you may visit http://www.gnuplot.org. A starting point to learn more about open-source software is The Open Source Initiative, http://www.opensource.org. Or try the Free Software Foundation, http://www.fsf.org, originators of the free-software movement.

P A R T

I

IN THE BEGINNING

Part I introduces the basic building blocks for techinical analysis using Bollinger Bands, discusses the importance of defining and using three different time frames in your operations, and presents the philosophical underpinnings of our work and approach to the markets.

1

INTRODUCTION

Over 80 years ago, the physicist Albert Einstein introduced his concept of relativity. At its core, relativity suggested that all things existed only in relation to one another. The inevitable conclusion is that nothing stands alone—there are no absolutes. For there to be black there must be white; fast exists only in relation to slow; a high cannot exist without a low for reference; etc. Einstein applied his theories to physics and in doing so lost a wider audience to whom those theories might have appealed. However, others such as the philosopher Bertrand Russell, were at work extending similar ideas beyond physics.

In a serialized form of his book [The ABC of Relativity] that appeared in The Nation *during 1925, Russell expressed the belief that once people had become used to the idea of relativity it would change the way they thought: people would work with greater abstraction and would replace old absolute laws with relative concepts. This has certainly happened in the world of science but the absorption of relativity into popular culture has done little to change the way most people think, simply because very few have got used to relativity or understand it in the least.*[1]

At about the same time Einstein was starting his work, Oliver Wendell Holmes, Jr., a U.S. Supreme Court justice, was engaged in pushing our nation's system of justice in the direction of relativity. He suggested that the courts could not determine absolute truth. They could only judge the relative merits of the competing claims before them, and they could not do so in an absolutist framework, but only in a framework relevant to society. Early in his career Holmes stated:

> *The law embodies the story of a nation's development through many centuries, and it cannot be dealt with as if it contained only the axioms and corollaries of a book of mathematics. In order to know what it is, we must know what it has been, and what it tends to become.*[2]

The work of Einstein and Holmes didn't stand alone. Their focus was an indication of an emerging trend within society. Since the world was starting to become more complex as the nineteenth century drew to a close, it was widely realized that the absolute truths that had governed the affairs of people would no longer serve, that a relative framework would be needed if progress were to continue—and so it is with the markets.

Such ideas are humble in their essence. They recognize our limits. They reflect Eastern rather than Western philosophy. The goal of the perfect approach to investing is just that, a goal. We may approach it, but it always will elude our grasp. Indeed, there is no perfect system. We can only do as well as we can within our limitations, at the urging of our potential.

Bernard Mandelbrot discovered nonlinear behavior in cotton prices in his early research into chaos. Others have followed who suggested that financial systems are in fact extremely complex, so complex that they exhibit hard-to-predict behavior similar to the best-known complex system, the weather. As systems become more complex, traditional linear analytical tools fail, and it becomes ever harder to understand them. The only tools that serve to help understand complex systems are relative tools.

It is not the purpose of this book to plumb the depths of the arguments, pro or con, regarding these matters. Rather, we accept the weight of the evidence that prices are not distributed normally and markets are not the simple systems that most people think they are. Our base assumption is that the markets are systems of increasing complexity that are ever harder to master.

The old saw suggests that in order to make money in the market, you must buy low and sell high—or vice versa. As the markets have become more volatile and the patterns more complex, this has become increasingly harder to do. There is a fable from the trading pits in Chicago where the most active of the world's futures contracts are traded. It suggests there is a god who rules the pits. This god has but two rules: One, you may buy the bottom tick—once in your life. Two, you may sell the top tick—again, once in your life. Of course, by implication you are free to do the opposite as often as you would like.

The purpose of this book is to help you avoid many of the common traps investors get caught in, including the buy-low trap where the investor buys only to watch the stock continue downward, or the sell-high trap, where the investor sells only to watch the stock continue upward. Here, the traditional, emotional approach to the markets is replaced with a relative framework within which prices can be evaluated in a rigorous manner leading to a series of rational investment decisions without reference to absolute truths. We may buy low, or sell high, but if we do so, we will do so only in a relative sense. References to absolutes will be minimized. The definition of *high* will be set as the upper trading band. The definition of *low* will be set as the lower trading band. In addition, there will be a number of suggestions to help you tune this framework to your individual preferences and adjust it to reflect your personal risk-reward criteria.

Part I starts with this chapter, the introduction. Then, in Chapter 2, you'll read about the raw materials available to the analyst. Next in Chapter 3, you'll learn how to select the proper time frames for your analysis and how to choose the correct length and width for Bollinger Bands. In a more philosophical vein, Chapter 4 looks at the contrasting approaches of continuous advice versus the process of locating setups that offer sup- erior risk-reward opportunities. Part I concludes with a discourse, in Chapter 5, on how to deploy successfully the ideas you will read about in this book.

Part II covers the technical details of Bollinger Bands. It begins with Chapter 6, on the history of trading bands (and in Chapter 20 in Part IV we reprise the oldest trading system known to us based on trading bands). Chapter 7, which describes the construction of Bollinger Bands, follows next. Chapter 8 is devoted to a discussion of the indicators that are derived from Bollinger Bands: %b, a method of mathematically determining whether we are high or low, and BandWidth, a measure of volatility. We close Part II with Chapter 9, which discusses volatility cycles, surveys some of the academic ideas that support the concept of Bollinger Bands, and reviews the relevant statistical issues.

If you are not interested in knowing the details behind the tools, you may want to skip Part II and go straight to Part III, where the discussion of how to use Bollinger Bands begins. While Parts III and IV build on the foundation laid out in the first two parts, you can read them independently.

Part III explains the basic use of Bollinger Bands. It starts with Chapters 10 and 11 on pattern recognition and introduces Arthur Merrill's M and W pattern categorization. Then Chapters 12 and 13 tackle the use of Bollinger Bands to clarify the most common trading patterns, with W bottoms covered in Chapter 12, and M tops explored in Chapter 13. The trickiest phase, "walking the bands," is taken up next, in Chapter 14. Finally there are two related chapters on volatility. Chapter 15 describes The Squeeze—with some examples for the stock and bond markets. Then Chapter 16 provides the first of three simple methods that illustrate the rigorous use of Bollinger Bands, a volatility-breakout system rooted in The Squeeze.

Part IV adds indicators to the analytical mix. It focuses on coupling bands and indicators in a rational decision-making framework. Chapter 17 offers a general discussion of coupling indicators and bands. Chapter 18 follows with a discussion of volume indicators, including those that are best suited for use with Bollinger Bands. In Chapter 19 and 20, we focus on combining price action and indicators in two rational decision systems using %b and volume oscillators—one system that follows trends and one that picks highs and lows.

Part V focuses on a couple of advanced topics, such as normalizing indicators with Bollinger Bands (Chapter 21) and techniques for day traders (Chapter 22), who are making increasing use of Bollinger Bands.

In Part VI, we summarize the major issues regarding Bollinger Bands via a list of rules and offer some closing thoughts.

Endnotes follow Part VI. Where I have had tangential thoughts that were important but that might interrupt the flow of the chapter, they have been included in the Endnotes. There is much of value in those notes and so be sure to check them out. The Endnotes also include references for material cited in the chapters.

The three trading methods presented in Parts III and IV are anticipatory in nature. Method I uses low volatility to anticipate high volatility. Method II uses confirmed strength to anticipate the beginning of an uptrend or confirmed weakness to anticipate the beginning of a downtrend. Method III anticipates reversals in two ways: by looking for weakening indicator readings accompanying a series of upper band tags or by looking for strengthening indicator readings accompanying a series of lower band tags. More dramatically, Method III also looks for nonconfirmed Bollinger Band tags, a tag of the lower band accompanied by a positive volume indicator or a tag of the upper band accompanying a negative volume indicator.

And now we turn our attention to jargon—you can't live with it and you can't live without it. Many years ago a new hotshot executive type at the Financial News Network, who came from radio and knew nothing of finance, declared that upon each and every use of jargon the presenter had to stop and define the term. He had a point. The terminology we used needed to be defined upon occasion, but not compulsively enough to halt the flow of content. A book allows for a convenient place where jargon can be slain, a Glossary. A lot of work went into keeping the use of jargon to a minimum and into the Glossary, so if you stumble across an unfamiliar term that is undefined in the text, or an unexpected usage, just turn to the Glossary and you'll most likely find the definition. The Glossary serves another purpose too. In many cases investing terminology is poorly defined. Terms may have more than one sense or multiple meanings, all of which can be confusing. In the Glossary the sense of the terms as used here is laid out.

The book closes with a Bibliography—really more of a suggested reading list that is closely coupled to the subject matter at hand. It is not meant to be a scholarly cross-reference to the literature; rather it is a useful guide to readily accessible relevant books. Most of the books should be available in your library or easily obtained from your favorite financial bookseller.

I have included a handy reference card for your convenience. It's bound into the back of the book. The basic Bollinger Bands rules are set out on the front of the card, the inside presents the M and W patterns, and the back presents the most important formulas. Tear it out and use it for a bookmark while you read. Then keep it by your computer so it is handy when you do your analysis.

Finally, we have built a Web site, http://www.BollingeronBollingerBands.com, to support *Bollinger on Bollinger Bands*. There you'll find daily lists of the stocks that qualify for each of the three methods presented here and a screening area where you can screen a large universe of stocks based on any of the criteria from this book. There is great charting, a community area where you can discuss the issues and ideas related to Bollinger Bands, and links to our other sites as well.

Upon finishing this book you will have at your disposal a set of tools and techniques that allow you to evaluate potential and actual investments and trades in a rigorous manner. This is an approach that allows you to eliminate much of the emotion surrounding the investing/trading process and therefore allows you to reach your true potential as an investor/trader.

2

THE RAW
MATERIALS

The market technician has a relatively small data set to work with, primarily price and volume. The data is reported for a chosen period—the high of the day, the low of the week, the volume for the hour, and so on. Typically the data comes in the form of date (time), open, high, low, close, and volume (see Table 2.1). The close is the most often consulted piece of data, followed by the high and low, then volume, and, last, the opening price. In June 1972, Dow Jones removed the opening prices from the *Wall Street Journal* in order to expand its listings and has never put them back. So several generations grew up without access to the open. Fortunately, with the advent of electronically distributed data, the open has again become widely available in the United States and is being used after a long period of neglect.

These basic data elements can be combined in a variety of ways to form the charts that traders and investors typically use.

Table 2.1 Typical Price Record for IBM*

Date	Open	High	Low	Close	Volume
19-Jan-01	107.50	113.9375	107.25	**111.25**	14,762,200
18-Jan-01	104.375	110	103.50	**108.3125**	25,244,900
17-Jan-01	95.375	97.75	94.3125	**96.6875**	9,727,000
16-Jan-01	93.75	94	91.8125	**92.75**	5,671,900
12-Jan-01	93.6875	96.4375	92.375	**93.8125**	6,448,000
11-Jan-01	92.9375	94.25	91.25	**93.6875**	9,635,000
10-Jan-01	92.50	94.9375	91.6875	**93.4375**	7,656,100

*From www.yahoo.com

There are four types of charts of significance: the line chart, the bar chart, the candlestick chart, and the point-and-figure chart. The line chart is the simplest of all, offering an outline of price action. The bar chart is the chart of choice in the West, usually drawn without the open or volume. Candlestick charts, which are rapidly gaining acceptance in the West, come from Japan, where they are the charting method of choice. Point-and-figure charts depict price action, pure and simple, and are perhaps the oldest of Western technical charting techniques.

Charts may be created for any time period: 10 minutes, hourly, daily, weekly, etc. Years ago the primary chart types were daily, weekly, and monthly. Hourly, daily, and weekly charts became the popular choice in the 1980s, and the trend has continued toward ever-shorter time periods, with tick charts that display each trade as well as five-minute and shorter charts enjoying ever-increasing greater popularity.

Most charts display price on the vertical, or y, axis, and time on the horizontal, or x, axis. But that is not always the case. EquiVolume charts—invented by Edwin S. Quinn and popularized by Richard Arms of Arms Index fame—depict volume on the x axis. Point-and-figure charts depict the number of price swings in excess of a given value on the x axis.

Line charts simplify the action greatly by taking a connect-the-dots approach and connecting the closes to render a sketch of the action.[1] Line charts often are used for clarity when a great deal of data must be displayed and bar charts or candlesticks would be too cluttered. They also are used when only a single point is available for each period, such as the daily advance-decline line or a value for an index calculated just once a day, as shown in Figure 2.1.

A conventional bar chart, shown in Figure 2.2, consists of a vertical line connecting the high and low with a horizontal tick to the left at the open and another horizontal tick to the right at

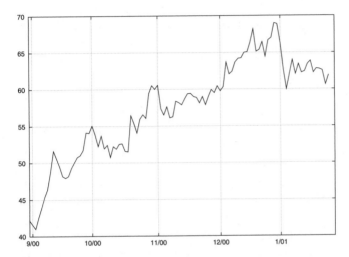

Figure 2.1 Line chart, Freddie Mac, 100 days. Note the lack of detail.

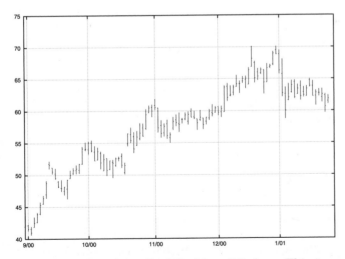

Figure 2.2 Bar chart, Freddie Mac, 100 days. This is a much better view of the action.

the close. When volume is included, it is usually plotted in a
separately scaled clip beneath the price clip as a histogram rising
from a baseline of zero. Each volume bar records the volume of
trade during the period depicted by the price bar immediately
above it. (Often the last two—or more—digits of volume are
omitted.)

Japanese candlestick charts place a greater emphasis on the
opening and closing prices than do bar charts. This is accomplished by drawing a narrow vertical box delineated by open and
close—the main body. The body is filled in (black) if the close is
lower than the open; otherwise it is left empty (white). From the
top and bottom of the box, thin line segments—the shadow lines—
are drawn to the high and low of the day if these points are outside
the box, as seen in Figure 2.3. I have employed candlestick charts
for many years and prefer them to bar charts; they create a clearer
picture for me.

Bollinger Bars (Figure 2.4) were created in an effort to
combine the advantages of both bar and candlestick charts.
Bollinger Bars are a cross between bar charts and candlestick
charts, where the portion of the bar between the open and the
close is colored red if the close is lower than the open or green
if the close is higher. The remainder of the bar is colored blue.

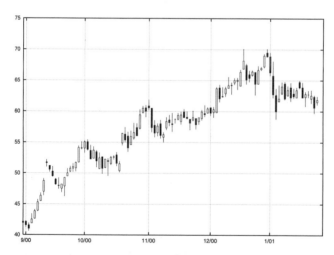

Figure 2.3 Candlestick chart, Freddie Mac, 100 days.
The important relationship between the open and the
close can now be seen clearly.

1/22 62.9380 +0.125

Freddie Mac

Copyright 2001 Acme Analytics
Rating History

09/14/2000 10/04/2000 10/24/2000 11/13/2000 12/04/2000 12/22/2000

Figure 2.4 Bollinger Bars, Freddie Mac, 90 days. This is a Western take on candlesticks.

These bars have the benefit of highlighting the important relationship between the open and close without taking up the extra space the candlesticks require. Bollinger Bars can be seen in action on http://www.EquityTrader.com.

Point-and-figure charts (Figure 2.5) reduce price action to its very essence, plotting rising columns of Xs when prices are strong and falling columns of Os when prices decline. No reference is made to time[2]; all that appears is price movement filtered by a combination of box-size and reversal rules. More information on this is given in Chapter 11, "Five-Point Patterns."

There are two main scaling techniques for the price axis. By far the most common is arithmetic scaling, where each division on the price axis is equidistant and represents an equal-point amount (Figure 2.6). Far more informative are log scales (Figure 2.7). In this system, sometimes referred to as ratio or semilog scaling, an equal distance at any point on the price axis represents an equal-percentage change, rather than an equal-point change. Thus equal-interval numbers appear closer together near the top of the chart than they do at the bottom. So 90 will be closer to 91 than 50 will be to 51. The beauty of log scaling is that it draws the eye toward a proper assessment of risk and reward without regard to price level. With an arithmetic scale a one-point move at $10 covers the same distance as a one-point move at $100, despite the fact that the

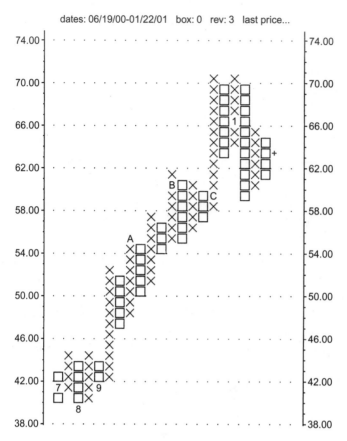

Figure 2.5 Point-and-figure chart, Freddie Mac, 120 days. Pure price action.

move was 10 percent at $10 and 1 percent at $100. With log scaling the one-point move covered only a tenth as much chart ground at $100 as it did at $10. Thus the gains and losses of equal visual magnitude are of equal value to the portfolio, no matter where they are represented on the chart. Log scaling is highly recommended.

The purpose of presenting bar charts and candlesticks, as well as arithmetic and logarithmic scales, is to allow you to make up your mind about which suits you better. However, let me make my preferences clear: In most circumstances I prefer log scales and Bollinger Bars.

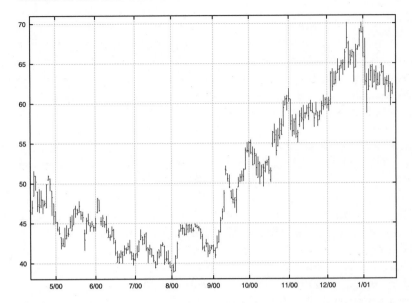

Figure 2.6 Bar chart, linear scale, Freddie Mac, 200 days. A point on the chart occupies an equal distance no matter what the price level.

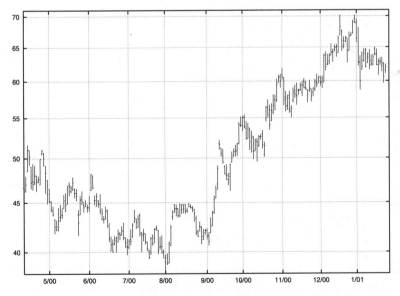

Figure 2.7 Bar chart, log scaling, Freddie Mac, 200 days. An equal distance on the chart indicates an equal percent change.

Normally volume is simply plotted beneath price in a separate clip as a histogram—that is, as lines drawn upward from a baseline typically set at zero (Figure 2.8). So it has been for many years, with only the occasional trend line or moving average drawn to create a frame of reference. And that is fine for as far as it goes, but it can be improved upon.

First, the use of a moving average of volume, traditionally a 50-day average, provides a consistent reference for whether volume is high or low (Figure 2.9). It is especially important to know whether volume is high or low on a relative basis when diagnosing M and W patterns (more on Ms and Ws in Part III). For example, most of the time volume will be higher on the left-hand side of a W bottom than on the right-hand side of the same formation.

Second, a reference to the average helps, but how do we compare across issues, or across markets? We do this by creating a relative measure. Divide volume by its 50-day moving average,[3] multiply the result by 100, and plot it in the same place and in the same way you would have plotted the regular volume histogram with a reference line drawn at 100 (Figure 2.10). Conceptually you have grabbed the ends of the moving average and pulled it straight. Thus volume above the reference line is greater than

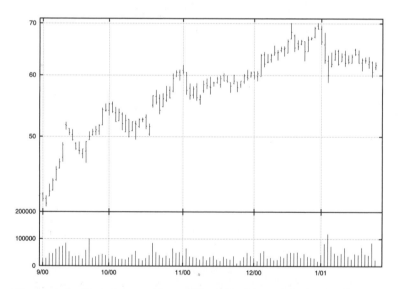

Figure 2.8   Bar chart, volume, Freddie Mac, 100 days. Plotting volume in a separate clip adds a new and important dimension.

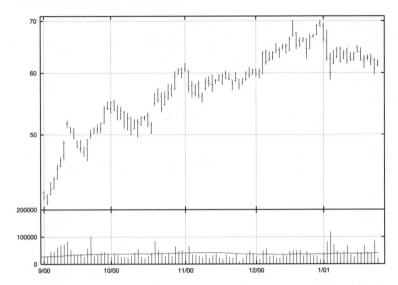

Figure 2.9 Bar chart, volume and average, Freddie Mac, 100 days. Adding a moving average to volume provides a definition of high and low volume.

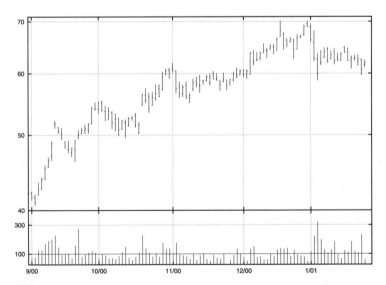

Figure 2.10 Bar chart, normalized volume, Freddie Mac, 100 days. Dividing volume by the moving average facilitates comparability.

Table 2.2   Additional Raw Materials for the Technician

Psychological indicators such as sentiment surveys, option-trading
  indicators, and futures premiums
Comparisons such as relative strength to the S&P and momentum
  rankings
Intermarket data depicting the relationships between related items
Transaction data such as bid and ask prices, the volume of each trade,
  and the exchange where traded
Structural data including industry groups and economic sectors
Firm-size data such as small cap versus large cap
Implied volatility
Valuation categorizations such as growth versus value

average, or strong, and volume below the reference line is less
than average, or weak.

Now you can compare volume across time, as well as across
markets. So you might determine that volume doubled; volume
was low; etc. Just as Bollinger Bands create a relative framework
for price, normalizing volume using the 50-day average creates a
relative framework for volume.

Finally, Table 2.2 presents some other raw materials for
technical analysis. Though they are important, they need not
concern us here; our focus is on price, volume, and volatility.

KEY POINTS TO REMEMBER

- Basic data include the open, high, low, close, and volume.
- Don't neglect the open.
- Four types of charts are line, bars, point and figure, and
  candlestick.
- Bollinger Bars are the marriage of bars and candlesticks.
- Log scaling is important.
- Normalize volume.

TIME FRAMES

Throughout this book three time frames are used: short, intermediate, and long. They are familiar terms, but they probably
convey unique meanings to you based on who you are and how
you trade. In one sense they can mean different things to different
investors; in another sense they convey similar psychological
concepts. Individual investors will imbue each term with their own
horizons, while at the same time organizing the various tasks and
functions according to time frame. Thus for one investor *long term*
will mean a year, while another will consider *long term* to mean
overnight. Yet at the same time these rather different investors will
find that they have organized their investing tasks in a similar
categorization of short-, intermediate-, and long-term tasks.

Up though the late seventies, *short term* referred to daily
charts, *intermediate term* to weekly charts, and *long term* to monthly
or quarterly charts. And while the charts were referred to this

Table 3.1   Possible Time Frame Combinations

Long Term	Intermediate Term	Short Term
Year	Quarter	Week
Quarter	Month	Week
Month	Week	Day
Week	Day	Hour
Day	Hour	10 minutes
Hour	10 minutes	Ticks

way, the terms really referred to the types of bars depicted on the charts, not to the charts themselves. Thus a short-term chart used daily bars by definition. In the early eighties, the pace of change started quickening. The demarcation was the introduction of stock index futures trading, with the birth of the ValueLine futures traded on the Kansas City Board of Trade. *Short term* started meaning hourly charts, *intermediate term* daily charts, and *long term* weekly or monthly charts. In the intervening years the trend has continued relentlessly toward ever-shorter time frames. See Table 3.1 for possible time frame combinations. However, no matter what the time frame, the underlying concepts are approximately the same.

For example, long term is the time frame in which you do your background analysis. It is the environment in which you determine your overall outlook and the broad strokes of your investment plan. For investors with long horizons, monetary and fiscal policy figure importantly, as does the flow of funds, valuation data, and the regulatory environment. For investors with a shorter horizon, important factors might be the direction of the 200-day average or the slope of the yield curve.

Intermediate term is the time frame in which you do your security analysis. It is the time frame for stock selection and group rotation. Broad market statistics can be important here. Long-horizon investors will consider broad market data such as advances and declines, new highs and lows, sector rotation, relative-strength trends, and quarterly supply and demand factors. Shorter-term investors may be looking at consolidations, turning points, and breakouts in industry groups.

Short term is the time frame in which you execute your trades. It is the time frame you use when placing your orders and seeing to the optimum execution of your strategy. This is usually the province of short-term technical indicators, price patterns, changes in volatility, trading data from the floor, etc.

Each time frame has its tasks, and those tasks, along with the tools used to accomplish them, will vary from investor to investor. What is most important is to keep each time frame's tasks separate and distinct. A prime example of breaking this rule is to continue looking at the short-term chart after the trade is executed! After execution, your focus should shift back to your intermediate-term tools, as these are the tools you maintain your trade with. Only when your intermediate-term tools and techniques call for exiting the trade, either to take a profit or to prevent further loss, should you turn back to your short-term tools to execute the decision.

The blurring of the tasks in combination with the mixing of time frames actually makes investing harder. It confuses the decision-making process and clouds thinking. Often when the time to make a critical decision is at hand, the temptation is the strongest to abandon discipline and use a tool or tools in a manner for which they were not intended. While this may seem to add information, the bottom line is less reliable information. The new data acts to muddy the waters with conflicting information not well matched to the task at hand.

From an analytical perspective, these ideas have important impacts. Bollinger Bands can be used in all three time frames. They can be scaled to suit in three ways, by choosing the time period represented by each bar, by choosing the number of bars used in the calculation, and by specifying the width of the bands. The base for Bollinger Bands ought to be a chart with bars coincident with your intermediate time frame, the base time frame for the calculation ought to be the average that is best descriptive of your intermediate-term trend, and the width ought to be a function of the length of the average. In our shop, daily bar charts, a 20-day calculation period, and 2 standard deviation bands are typical.

Note the use of the term *descriptive* in the paragraph above. Do not try to pick the average that gives the best crossover buy and sell signals. In fact, the average we want is considerably longer than the average picked by an optimizer looking for the greatest profit from crossover signals. Why is this? Because our signals will come from interaction with the bands, not from crossovers. The average we select is used as a base for building a relative framework within which we can evaluate price action in a rigorous manner. This average will be better at defining support and resistance than at providing crossover signals.

The best way to identify the correct average is to look for the average that provides support to reactions, especially the first reaction after a change in trend. Suppose the market makes a low, rallies for 10 days, and then pulls back for 5 days before turning higher again and confirming the birth of the new uptrend by taking out the high for the initial 10-day rally. The correct average would be the one that offered support at the low of the 5-day pullback (Figure 3.1). An average that was too long would have been too slow to define support, and too slow in turning higher to describe the new trend (Figure 3.2). An average that was too short would have been crossed three or more times, and would not have given useful support or trend information (Figure 3.3).

In studies done many years ago, the 20-day average proved to be a good starting point for most things financial. The adaptivity of Bollinger Bands comes primarily from volatility, not from moving-average length selection; so we want an average length

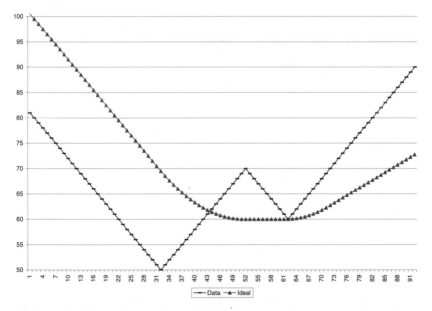

Figure 3.1 Moving average, correct. Price crosses the average shortly after the low and then provides support on the first pullback.

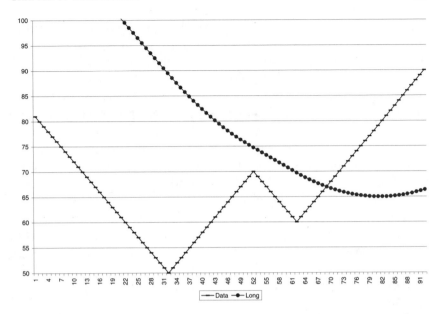

Figure 3.2   Moving average, too long. Price crosses the average too late.

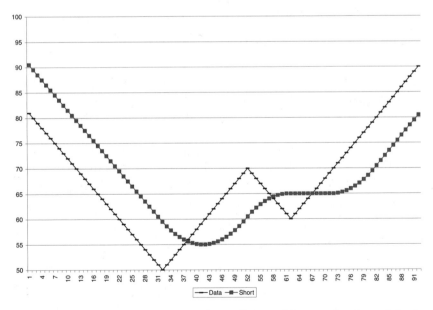

Figure 3.3   Moving average, too short. Price whipsaws back and forth across the average.

long enough to capture intermediate-term trend and volatility information.[1]

It turns out that as you vary the length of the moving average, you also need to vary the number of standard deviations used to plot the bands. A 20-period average provides a good base for most applications, but some series require longer or shorter time periods. A bandwidth of ±2 standard deviations provides an equally good starting point, but again we find the need for variation. Some variation is a function of average length, and some is a function of the width of the bands. Table 3.2 presents the parameters for daily charts that have been recommended over the years and have been deployed successfully by many traders.

In doing the research for this book, we conducted a study that suggests that the need to vary the bands according to average length has diminished in today's marketplace. The study, and the parameters now recommended, is presented in Chapter 7 on construction in Part II.

Interestingly enough, the Bollinger Band construction rules have held together pretty well over the years and across the markets. The original construction rules and parameters have been consistently effective, suggesting that they are quite robust. Further evidence of the robustness of the base parameters comes from the fact that small changes to the parameters do not produce large changes in the systems in which they are used. This insensitivity to small changes[2] is very important in designing a system that will prove useful over time.

It doesn't seem to make much difference what the bar types are—daily, 10 minute, etc. However, traders using very short-term bars tend to use narrower bandwidths than might be expected. This may be because many of these traders are using Bollinger

Table 3.2 Traditional Parameters for the Width of Bollinger Bands

Periods	Multiplier
10	1.5
20	2.0
50	2.5

Bands as a type of volatility breakout system. We will go into this more in Chapter 22 on day trading.

KEY POINTS TO REMEMBER

- Three time frames are short, intermediate, and long.
- Fit the time frames to your own horizons.
- Organize tasks by time frame.
- Use a descriptive average as a base.

4

CONTINUOUS ADVICE

Seamless guidance across time is highly sought after by investors; no investment system or plan renders continuous advice, though many purport to do so. This is true whether the system is fundamental, technical, or some blend of the two, or whether it is one of the famous investment plans from the past[1] or one of the new-fangled programs of today. There may be times when a system is working well, but inevitably the time will come when it is working poorly or not at all. There may be markets in which it is effective, just as there may be markets for which it is ill suited.[2]

Mutual fund investors seem to be the group that spends the most time chasing the holy grail of continuous advice, mostly via the various switching programs. Some programs switch in and out of just one fund, while others switch from fund to fund or sector to sector. Some programs continuously alter the balance of a portfolio of funds. Some approaches seek out the highest-performing funds, whereas others try to achieve some stable rate of return while attempting to reduce or eliminate risk. All share one factor in common: The system is deployed and relied on continuously.

And eventually, for all, disaster strikes. It is inevitable. Markets change, economies change, and the world changes. Waves of panic and greed sweep through the markets. Rules and regulations change. The infrastructure changes. Fund managers and fund objectives change, sometimes without notice. And then there are subtle changes that are only understood and recognized after the fact—sometimes long after the fact. All this conspires to render any system of continuous advice moot after a while—sometimes after only a very short while. No amount of testing or planning for change can alter this.

Perhaps most important of all, even if the foregoing were not true, investors change. The plan that fits today chafes tomorrow. Yesterday's goals become today's irrelevancies. Today's plans become tomorrow's noise. Age changes; income changes; needs and desires change. A plan to be relied on today becomes an adversary tomorrow. And even if the investor could remain constant, relative change occurs; the economy evolves and changes the environment the investor lives, works, and invests in.

No system, program, or investment plan can survive this onslaught of change. This is true regardless of how well thought out or adaptive it is. Baron Rothschild asserted that the simplest system, compound interest, was the eighth wonder of the world, and then pointed out that not even that approach could be relied upon. Taxes interfere; banks collapse; capital is confiscated; wars intervene; governments change; jail looms; the public objects; socialism arrives. ... It is no accident that the annual tabulation of the world's richest people is composed mostly of people who made their fortunes, not those who inherited—generating wealth is far easier than preserving it.

The point is not that we are without hope; it is just that continuous advice is not a viable alternative. What is viable is discrete advice—the identification of individual opportunities with superior risk-reward characteristics that can be exploited. Those discrete opportunities can be woven into approaches that can be adapted over time to reach one's goals. It is to this effort that this book is dedicated.

Many people expect that Bollinger Bands alone, or perhaps even with the use of indicators, can and will deliver continuous advice about what to do. They open up a chart, and after a quick scan they focus on the right-hand side—where the most recent price bars are—and try to decide what action to take. If an appropriate setup is at hand, their chances of success are good. If not, their chances are at best no better than random and perhaps a bit worse, for emotions will rule. This is a flawed approach that eventually will lead to trouble.

What works is the identification of individual opportunities with superior risk-reward characteristics. These may occur frequently, several times a year in a given stock, or not at all. Our job is to find and exploit these patterns when they appear. This means sifting through a number of stocks, funds, indices, etc., looking for opportunity. Often one can look at a chart and see that what to do is clear. More often it is not clear. We must be like a forty-niner panning for gold. That does not mean continuously panning whether there is gold to be found or not. It means finding the right time and place and then going to work.

In order to help you locate these opportunities we have set up a Web site, http://www.BollingeronBollingerBands.com. Waiting there for you are daily lists of the stocks that qualify under each of the methods presented in this book. These lists have been prescreened from a large universe of stocks. If you prefer to do your own screening, there is a stock screener that will let you screen for opportunities based on any of the criteria from this book.

The focus in this book is on identifying opportunities using Bollinger Bands and indicators. This book offers not a panacea, but a set of tools and techniques. It says in Ecclesiastes, "To every thing there is a season, and a time to every purpose under the heaven." So too it is in investing. These tools and techniques each have their times and uses. Carefully and thoughtfully deployed, these tools can help you achieve your goals, at least insofar as they are achievable.

KEY POINTS TO REMEMBER

- Continuous advice doesn't work.
- Bollinger Bands can help find setups with good risk-reward characteristics.
- Indicators can help.
- Technical and fundamental analysis can be combined to your advantage.

5

BE YOUR OWN MASTER

Throughout this book many different concepts are presented and rules given. Time frames are inferred, indicators are recommended, and approaches are discussed. In some places the recommendations are quite specific and in others deliberately vague. All have one thing in common: You must suit yourself if you are to be successful.

One investor will be able to withstand only very small losses before having to exit, whereas another will be much more tolerant of short-term volatility in seeking intermediate- or long-term gains. Currently in vogue among momentum investors is a rule that suggests exiting if a 7 or 8 percent loss is encountered. Nothing could be more absurd, for investors must determine for themselves the discipline they must follow. While an 8 percent stop-loss rule might work well for some investors, it might keep others from making money at all, or even cause them to lose money. There are no ironclad rules that work across a broad spectrum of investors.

Here are two examples that demonstrate how investors bend existing frameworks to suit their needs:

A Web site I created that analyzes stocks, www.EquityTrader.com, presents Performance and Potential ratings. The Performance ratings are risk-adjusted, front-weighted, historical performance measures suitable for intermediate-term forecasting based on daily charts. The Potential ratings are derived from a fuzzy logic model employing both technical and fundamental rules, and are shorter term in nature—more traders' tools than investors' tools. Communications from users suggest that they are picking and choosing among the various EquityTrader (ET) tools, in some cases combining them to create unique approaches to using ET for profit. That is exactly the right idea.

Futures Truth, and other organizations of similar stripe, tests and reports on the profitability and characteristics of many trading systems that are offered for sale to the public. Users who buy those systems most often find that their results differ from what they had expected, sometimes markedly. This illustrates an old truism. Teach a dozen investors a trading system, and when you come back a year later, you'll find a dozen systems. For various reasons the users will have tweaked—perhaps massively—the system to fit their own needs. Thus virtually any system can be taught widely with little fear of its effectiveness being diluted.[1]

To be successful, investors must learn to think for themselves. This is true because they are unique individuals with varying goals and differing risk and reward criteria. Investors must fashion an investment program that not only is profitable, but is one they will be able to execute. No system—however profitable—will work for them if they are unable to follow it. The idea that only a custom-tailored approach has any real chance of success is as close to a universal truth about investing as it is possible to get.

Independence and independent thinking are the keys. It is very comfortable to go with the crowd and do as others are doing—or as they tell you to do. Yet this is a road fraught with peril. Consider Robert Frost's "The Road Not Taken."

> *Two roads diverged in a yellow wood,*
> *And sorry I could not travel both*

And be one traveler, long I stood
And looked down one as far as I could
To where it bent in the undergrowth;

Then took the other, as just as fair,
And having perhaps the better claim,
Because it was grassy and wanted wear;
Though as for that the passing there
Had worn them really about the same,

And both that morning equally lay
In leaves no step had trodden black.
Oh, I kept the first for another day!
Yet knowing how way leads on to way,
I doubted if I should ever come back.

I shall be telling this with a sigh
Somewhere ages and ages hence:
Two roads diverged in a wood, and I—
I took the one less traveled by,
And that has made all the difference.

Your path, created, maintained, and traveled by yourself, will be that path less traveled, for it will be yours and yours alone; no one else will be able to follow it, just as you will be unable to follow anyone else's path successfully. You do not share their vision, their sensitivities, or their cares, and they do not share yours. In investing, there is no holy grail other than the one you fashion for yourself.

KEY POINTS TO REMEMBER

- Think for yourself.
- Know your risk tolerance.
- Know your goals.
- Follow your own path.
- Be disciplined.

II
P A R T

THE BASICS

Part II lays out the basics of Bollinger Bands. Chapters 6, 7, and 8 examine the history of trading bands and envelopes, the construction of the Bollinger Bands, and the indicators derived from them, respectively. Finally, Chapter 9 looks at statistics, for those interested in the deus ex machina.

6

HISTORY

The history of trading bands, envelopes, channels, etc., is long and interesting. Only the highlights are covered here, enough to provide you with an idea of the origins of the craft and a sense of perspective.[1]

Perhaps it is best to start with definitions. *Trading bands* are bands constructed above and below some measure of central tendency—for example, a moving average shifted up and down by some percentage of itself. Bands need not be symmetrical, but they do reference some central point. *Envelopes* are constructed around the price structure, above a moving average of the highs and below a moving average of the lows, for example. Envelopes may be symmetrical, but most often they are asymmetrical and do not refer to a central point. *Channels* are parallel lines drawn around prices such that the channels touch the price structure at key points.

The earliest citation we have uncovered comes from Wilfrid LeDoux, who copyrighted in 1960 the Twin-Line Chart (Figure 6.1). A simple but elegant approach, it called for connecting the monthly highs with a black line and the monthly lows with a red line. Several rules were given, the clearest of which called for a buy when the red line (monthly lows) exceeded a trough made by the black line (monthly highs) by two points. The idea of this technique was to clarify chart patterns that resulted in major swings to help time one's operations in a given stock with maximum efficiency. We have not tested this technique, but the examples we have seen suggest it works admirably.

Mr. LeDoux commenced operations in 1918 and was wiped out by 1921, an unfortunate occurrence that led to his research. The first tools he employed, circa 1930, were his ROBOT charts, called Detectographs, which also focused on highs relative to lows and vice versa, though a technique we have been unable to uncover. Unfortunately, we are also unable to discover the precise time he started deploying channels. Suffice it to say that it had to be prior to the publication of the Twin-Line Chart in 1960.

LeDoux's use of monthly charts is quite striking. Clearly, this points to the long-term orientation that was more prevalent in his day. At that time, the terms *overbought* and *oversold* were used exclusively to refer to long-term, climactic tops and bottoms, exactly the types of events that one would be able to observe clearly on monthly charts. This is especially interesting in light of the broad use of these terms today to apply to the shortest possible time frames. The markets clearly do evolve.

At about the same time LeDoux copyrighted his Twin-Line technique, Chester W. Keltner hinted at things to come when he published the Ten-Day Moving Average Rule in his 1960 book *How to Make Money in Commodities* (see Figure 6.2). Keltner began by calculating the typical price—add the high, low, and close for a given period and divide by three.[2] He then took a 10-day moving average of the typical price and plotted it on the chart. Next he calculated a 10-day average of the daily range (high-low). In downtrends he calculated and plotted a line equal to the 10-day average of the typical price *plus* the 10-day average of the range. This was the buying line, the line where you covered your short position and went long (reversing your position from short to long). In uptrends the average of the daily range was *subtracted*

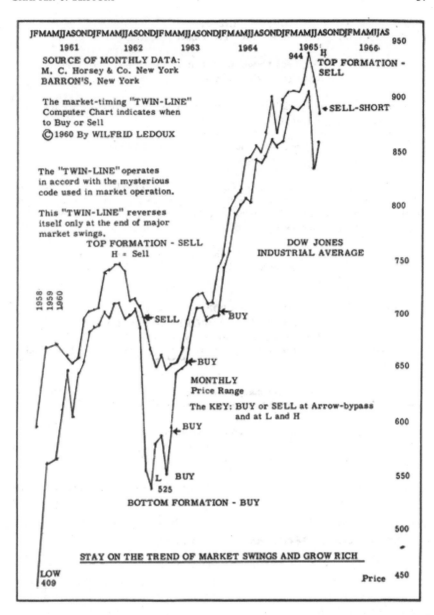

Figure 6.1 Twin-Line Chart, an early example of trading envelopes. (SOURCE: *The Encyclopedia of Stock Market Techniques*, New Rochelle, N.Y.: Investors Intelligence, 1985.)

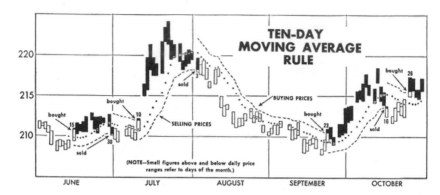

Figure 6.2 Keltner Buy and Sell Lines. The buying and selling prices can be combined to form bands. (SOURCE: *How to Make Money in Commodities* by Chester W. Keltner, Kansas City, Mo.: The Keltner Statistical Service, 1960.)

Table 6.1 Keltner Band Formulas

Keltner Buy Line:
  10-day-moving-average typical price + 10-day moving average (high-low)

Keltner Sell Line:
  10-day-moving-average typical price − 10-day moving average (high-low)

from the average of the typical price to produce a selling line. When the price fell below the selling line, you closed any long positions and sold short (reversing your position from long to short). See Table 6.1 for a summary of Keltner's formulas.

Keltner's techniques are significant in several ways:

First, the use of the typical price was insightful. The typical price gives a better feel for the price where the majority of trading usually occurs than does the most commonly used price, the close or last. By including the opening price, the typical price also picks up some reference to the activity that occurred between sessions. This is especially useful in today's markets where the quote you get may not cover all the significant trading activity in that period. For example, a quote on an NYSE stock will usually reflect the NYSE session, and may or may not include off-exchange or after-hours trading. In addition, significant activity occurs over-seas, which may or may not overlap the primary session covered by your quote. For simplicity and clarity in this book, we will use the close, but we urge you to consider employing the typical price in your operations.

Second, Keltner's use of the daily range to determine the interval between the average and the band foreshadowed the more fully adaptive methods that were taken up later. The daily range also incorporates an aspect of volatility into the process, which we think is crucial to success.

Third, if both the buy and sell lines were projected simulta-neously and continuously, rather than in Keltner's checkerboard or alternating fashion, you would have what might have been the first example of a trading band (Figure 6.3) in the sense that became popular later.

In the 1960s Richard Donchian took the simple, but elegant, approach of letting the market set its own trading envelopes via his four-week rule. The concept was simplicity itself. One bought

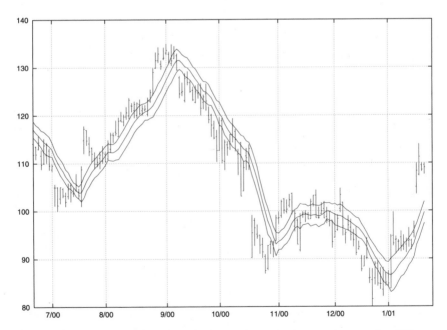

Figure 6.3 Keltner Channel, IBM, 150 days. Keltner's buy and sell lines combined to form trading bands.

when the four-week high was exceeded and sold when the four-week low was broken. In a subsequent test of computerized trading systems, this rule was selected to be the best of many tested by Dunn & Hargitt, a well-respected commodity trading and analytics firm of the time.

The four-week rule was soon turned into envelopes by drawing lines equal to the highest high of the past four weeks and the lowest low of the past four weeks. This concept of setting the upper limit at the *n*-period high and the lower limit at the *n*-period low is often referred to today as a *Donchian Channel* (Figure 6.4). This concept is rumored to be at the heart of one of the more successful trading approaches in wide use today, that employed by the Turtles.[3]

In 1966, *Investment Quality Trends* (*IQT*), an investment newsletter edited by Geraldine Weiss, introduced a new type of envelope, the valuation envelope (Figure 6.5). Using an historical perspective, *IQT* presented monthly charts that included overvaluation and undervaluation lines based on dividend yield.

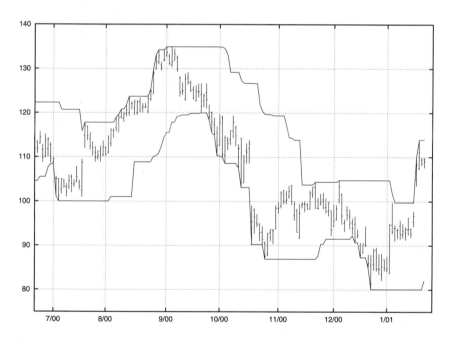

Figure 6.4 Donchian Channel, IBM, 150 days. This is a very popular approach with commodity traders.

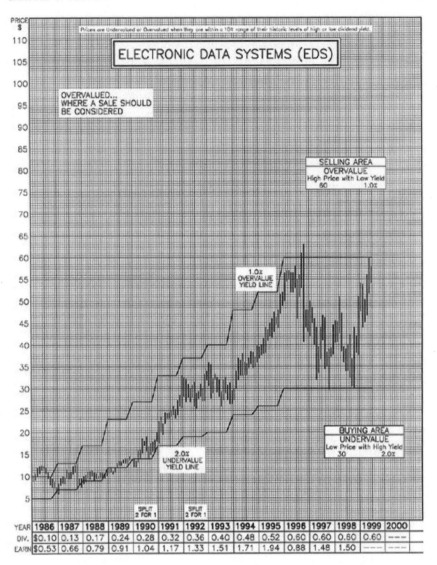

Figure 6.5 Valuation envelope, fundamental and technical analysis combined, Electronic Data Systems (EDS). (SOURCE: Investment Quality Trends, La Jolla, California.)

As we understand it, *IQT* uses the high and low yields achieved during a strategic base period as benchmarks to project future overvaluation and undervaluation levels based on then-current dividends. For a stock with growing dividends this envelope resembles a rising megaphone—a cone that widens as time passes. This was an early form of Rational Analysis, a concept we have defined as "the juncture of the sets of technical analysis and fundamental analysis." Indeed, Ms. Weiss was a pioneer. At the time, few newsletters took a rigorous quantitative approach. It must have been a lot of work in the days before computer power was widely available.

The next major development came in 1970 when J. M. Hurst published *The Profit Magic of Stock Transaction Timing*. Hurst's interest was in cycles, and he used "constant width curvilinear channels" to clarify the cyclic patterns in stocks. His approach was to use multiple hand-drawn envelopes (see Figure 6.6) that related to the various cyclic components of price action. The envelopes nested inside one another, often becoming congruent at major turning points. In the back of his book, he gave some broad hints at how this process might be mechanized (see Figure 6.7) but the examples presented in the text appear to be hand-drawn.

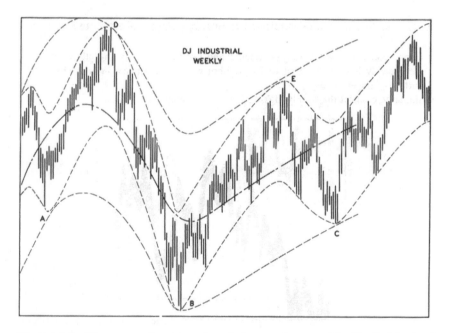

Figure 6.6 These envelopes are hand drawn. (SOURCE: *The Profit Magic of Stock Transaction Timing* by J. M. Hurst, 1970, reprinted by Traders Press, Greenville, S.C.)

Figure 6.7 Shows cycles used to help draw the envelopes. (SOURCE: *The Profit Magic of Stock Transaction Timing* by J. M. Hurst, 1970, reprinted by Traders Press, Greenville, S.C.)

We suspect that the concepts were beyond the technology then commonly available. In the years since, numerous attempts have been made to systematize Hurst's work, but we are not aware of any successful results.[4]

The development path of trading bands gets a bit murky here, and credit is hard to assign. In the next phase, interest seems to have broadened, and several analysts appear to have been working on similar ideas at the same time. The main technique employed in this phase was to shift a moving average in a parallel manner up and down to form bands around price (Figure 6.8). The offset was typically a number of points or a percentage of the average. See, for example, Table 6.2. Hurst had clearly favored the use of moving averages in his book, but we think the idea of shifting the averages by some mechanical means came later, perhaps in the early 1970s. The problems of this approach became apparent immediately. First, the width had to be determined empirically on an issue-by-issue basis. Second, even having done that, the widths needed adjustment over time. Thus, while

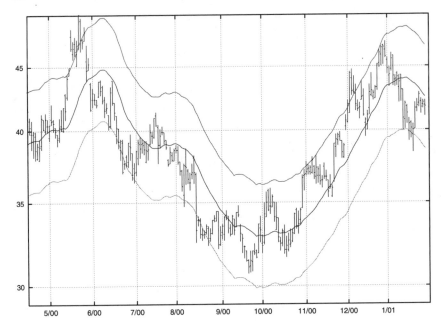

Figure 6.8 Stock with percentage envelopes, Deere & Co., 200 days. These are the earliest "modern" bands: percentage bands.

Table 6.2 Percentage Band Formulas
for 5 Percent Bands

Upper band = 21-day moving average * 1.05
Middle band = 21-day moving average
Lower band = 21-day moving average / 1.05

percentage or point bands did provide useful definitions of high and low for traders, they were hard to use and involved considerable guesswork on the part of the user.

In the early 1980s, William Schmidt of Tiger Software published a computerized black-box system for timing the market entitled *Peerless Stock Market Timing*. Many types of signals were generated. One aspect of the system used percentage bands (Figure 6.9). Signals were generated by comparing the action of indicators with price action within percentage moving-average bands. Some signals for the market as a whole involved the Dow Jones Industrial Average and breadth oscillators,[5] and some

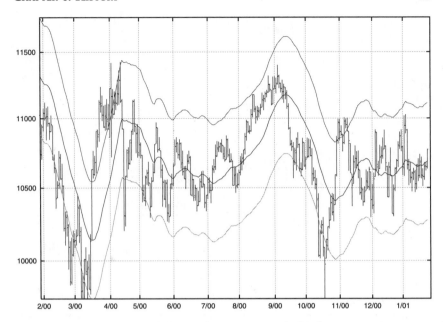

Figure 6.9   Dow Jones Industrial Average with 21-day moving average and 4 percent bands. Many a market timing system was built on percentage bands drawn around the Dow Jones Industrial Average.

signals for stocks involved volume oscillators. This work was indicative of a broad trend to systematize decision making using technical analysis.

Up to this point, all approaches to bands and envelopes were symmetrical. In the early 1980s, Marc Chaikin working with Bob Brogan produced the first fully adaptive bands. Called Bomar Bands (BOb and MARc), these were trading bands that contained 85 percent of the price action over the past year, as you can see in Table 6.3. The importance of this achievement cannot be

Table 6.3   Bomar Band Formulas

Bomar Bands
Upper band contains 85 percent of data above the average for the past 250
   periods
Middle band = 21-day moving average
Lower band contains 85 percent of data beneath the average for the past
   250 periods

Figure 6.10   Bomar Bands. (SOURCE: Instinet's Research and Analytics.)

overstated. In strong uptrends the upper Bomar Band would widen appropriately while the lower Bomar Band contracted. Volatile stocks had wide bands, whereas stable stocks had narrow bands. In downtrends the lower band expanded and the upper contracted (Figure 6.10). Thus, Bomar Bands not only broke with the idea that bands should be symmetrical but evolved over time to suit the price structure.

The major benefit conferred by Bomar Bands was that analysts were no longer forced to provide their own guesses about what the proper values for the bands were. Instead, they were free to focus on decision making and let their PCs set the bandwidth for them. Unfortunately, Bomar Bands were extremely computationally intensive for their time, and to this day are not readily available beyond Instinet's research and analytics (R&A) platform. Thus they have not achieved the broad acceptance they deserve.

The late Jim Yates of DYR Associates, working in the late 1970s and early 1980s, provided an important insight using implied volatility from the options market. He derived a method of determining whether a security was overbought or oversold in relation to market expectations. Mr. Yates showed that expectations of volatility could be used to create a framework within which one could make rational decisions regarding stocks and or options. This framework consisted of six zones and mapped out the appropriate option strategies for each zone (Figure 6.11). This became his Options Strategy Spectrum, which remains a useful tool to this day under the care of his son Bill.

What Jim did was to create zones (bands) based on the implied volatility of options. Then he used those bands to determine what strategies were most appropriate given market conditions. It was a brilliant insight that foreshadowed much of the work I was to do.

As the 1980s dawned, I was active in the options markets, the key to which is an understanding of volatility in its many forms, though I was not fortunate enough to have met Jim Yates yet. I also was very interested in technical analysis and specifically in trading bands. It occurred to me that the key to the proper bandwidth was volatility. So I embarked on a testing program that examined various measures of volatility as a method of setting bandwidth. It became readily apparent that the standard deviation calculation provided a superior result. This is primarily due to the squaring of the deviations from the average in the calculation.[6]

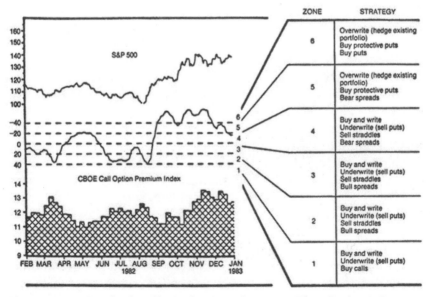

Figure 6.11 Implied risk indicator. (SOURCE: *The Options Strategy Spectrum* by James Yates, Homewood, Ill.: Dow Jones–Irwin, 1987.)

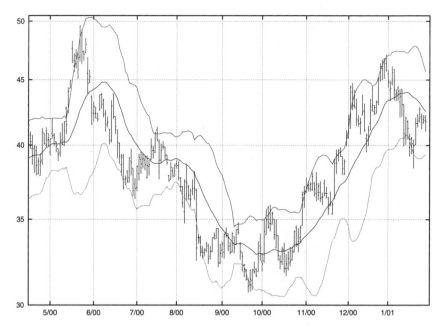

Figure 6.12   Bollinger Bands, Deere & Co., 200 days.

Initially, I calculated long-term standard deviation and used it to set percentage bands—in essence an adaptive version of percentage bands and still interesting in certain applications. However, as time passed, the settings drifted out of sync, entailing recalibration. It was then that I had the insight that standard deviation might be calculated in a "moving" manner just as we calculated a moving average (see Figure 6.12). The rest came quickly.

The development work on Bollinger Bands was done on an S-100 computer with 32 kilobytes of memory. The operating system used was a CP/M from Digital Research; the programming language was MBASIC, Bill Gates's first Microsoft product. Testing was done in a spreadsheet called SuperCalc. All of this took place in the days before the now-ubiquitous PC, when giants like IBM and Digital Equipment ruled the earth and the Apple Macintosh was but a gleam in Job's and Wozniac's eyes.

In the years since the creation of Bollinger Bands, several other attempts have been made to create adaptive bands, but none seem to have the vibrancy and usefulness of Bollinger Bands. Needless to say, I am very pleased by the wide acceptance my eponymous bands have received. While the rapid acceptance of Bollinger Bands was in part due to the airing they received on the Financial News Network, where I served as chief market analyst from 1983 through 1990, Bollinger Bands were the right tool at the right time, a tool that met a need that was simply not addressed by any other method.

If you ever wonder how Bollinger Bands got their name, this is the story. I had been using them for some time without having named them. One day I used a chart that depicted them in an on-air segment hosted by Bill Griffeth, who, in his usual forthright manner, asked what they were called as I explained their use. There you have it—on air, unprepared, at a loss, and out came Bollinger Bands.

KEY POINTS TO REMEMBER

- Bands have a long history.
- Many analysts have made important contributions.
- Percentage bands were most common.
- Bollinger Bands were born in 1983.
- The key to Bollinger Bands is volatility.
- Adaptivity is very important.

7

CONSTRUCTION

The construction of trading bands is really quite straightforward. You start with some measure of central tendency and build the bands above and below that measure. The questions are, What measure of central tendency should be used and what determines the interval? For Bollinger Bands the measure of central tendency is a simple moving average, and the interval is delineated by a measure of volatility, a moving standard deviation.

What does *moving* mean here? It means that for each period the analysis is calculated anew. For a moving average, each period's values are drawn from the immediately prior values. For a 20-day average, the most recent 20 days are used. The next day the oldest day's data is discarded and the newest included. The same is true for volatility; for each period, the volatility is measured using the immediately preceding periods.

How does this relate to trading bands or price envelopes? To my mind, trading bands are constructed above and below some central point, usually an average. Envelopes are constructed without reference to a central point—for example, moving averages of the highs and lows or curves fit around key highs and lows à la Hurst.

When it comes to trading bands, the problems are clear. The widths for percentage bands have to be changed from issue to issue in order to work; even for the same issue the bandwidth has to be changed as time passes in order to remain effective. Marc Chaikin had shown us one method of estimating the proper bandwidth; his Bomar Bands shifted a 21-day moving average up and down so that they contained 85 percent of the data over the past year. While this served his purposes well, for our purposes the price structure evolves more dynamically than the long look-back period of Bomar Bands allows for. Experiments in shortening the Bomar Band calculation period suggested that the calculations break down in short time frames. Marc Chaikin had hit the nail on the head with his decision to consult the market regarding the proper bandwidth, but what was needed was something that was more directly adaptive.

My first interest in the securities world was options. Analysis of options, whether options embedded in convertible bonds, warrants, or listed options, all turned on the same issue, volatility—specifically, an estimate of future volatility. The key to winning in that game was simple to grasp—but hard to use; you had to understand volatility better than the next person. Indeed, volatility seemed to be the key to many things, and so I studied volatility in all its forms: historical estimates, future estimates, statistical measurements, etc. When it came to trading bands, it was clear that in order to achieve success, the bands would have to incorporate volatility.

Once volatility was identified as the best way to set the width of trading bands, there were still a lot of choices. Volatility can be measured in many ways: as a function of the range over some period of time, as a measure of dispersion around a trend line, as the deviation from the expected—the list is literally endless.[1] After an initial scan, a list of seven candidate measures was settled upon. Early in the decision process it became clear that the more adaptive the approach, the better it would work. Of all the measures examined, standard deviation (sigma, σ) stood out in this regard.

To calculate standard deviation you first measure the average of the data set and then subtract that average from each of the points in the data set. The result is a list of the deviations from the average—some negative, some positive. The more volatile the series, the greater the dispersion of the list. The next step is to sum the list. However, the list as is will total to zero, because the pluses will offset the minuses. In order to measure the dispersion it is necessary to get rid of the negative signs. This can be done simply by canceling the minus signs. The resulting measure, mean absolute deviation, was one of the calculations that were initially considered. Squaring the members of the list also eliminates the negative numbers—a negative number multiplied by a negative number is a positive number—that's the method used in standard deviation. The last steps are easy—having squared the list of deviations, calculate the average squared deviation[2] and take the square root (see Table 7.1).

Table 7.1 The Population Formula for Standard Deviation

$$\sigma = \sqrt{\frac{\sum (x_i - \mu)^2}{N}}$$

where
x = data point
μ = the average
N = the number of points

While squaring the deviations has the benefit of allowing the rest of the computation to proceed, it also has a side effect: The deviations are magnified. In fact, the larger the deviation, the larger the magnification. There lies the key. For as prices surge or collapse and the deviations from the average grow, the squaring process inside the standard deviation calculation magnifies them and the bands efficiently adapt to the new prices. As a result it almost seems as if the bands chase after price. Do not underestimate this quality. It is the *key* to the bands' power to clarify patterns and maintain useful definitions of what is high and what is low.

The defaults for Bollinger Bands are a 20-day calculation—approximately the number of trading days in a month—and ±2 standard deviations. You will find that as you shorten the calculation period, you will need to reduce the number of standard deviations used to set the bandwidth, and that as you lengthen the number of periods, you will need to widen the bandwidth, as discussed below (or via the traditional method discussed in Chapter 4 of Part I).

The reason for the adjustment has to do with the standard deviation calculation itself. With a sample size of 30 or greater, ±2 standard deviations should contain about 95 percent of the data. With a sample size of less than 30, we really shouldn't be using the term *standard deviation*, but the calculation is sufficiently robust that it works anyway.[3] In fact, the bands contain near the amount of data one would expect them to all the way down to a sample size of 10. But one has to allow for changes in the bandwidth parameter as the calculation period shrinks and the results of the calculation change character to keep the containment constant.

The traditional approach to this was to use the data presented in Table 3.2, scaling the bandwidth between 1.5 and 2.5 standard deviations as the calculation period increased from 10 to 50. However, in preparing this book, a number of markets were tested to see whether that table still held true. It turns out that much smaller adjustments need to be made these days. Six markets were tested: IBM, the S&P 500 Index, the Nikkei 225 Index, gold bullion, the German mark/U.S. dollar cross rate, and the NASDAQ Composite. Ten years of data was used for everything except the mark, for which eight years of data was used. We calculated 10-, 20-, 30-, and 50-period Bollinger Bands. The bandwidth for all was then set to contain 89 percent of the data points, the average amount contained by the 20-day bands for all six series.[4]

The test results between the markets were very consistent. Based on those test results, as a general rule I recommend that if you use a starting point of 2 standard deviations and a 20-period calculation, you should decrease the bandwidth to 1.9 standard deviations at 10 periods and increase it to 2.1 standard deviations at 50 periods (see Table 7.2).

These adjustments are dramatically smaller than those previously recommended. There are likely numerous factors at work, a larger sample size and a better testing methodology or

Table 7.2 Recommended Width
Parameters for Bollinger Bands

Periods	Multiplier
10	1.9
20	2.0
50	2.1

platform, for example. But none is more important than the evolution of the markets. The initial Bollinger Band parameters were developed almost 20 years ago, and the markets have changed dramatically since then. For example, stock index futures were new, unproven vehicles at the time. There can be no doubt that the markets have evolved since then, and our approaches need to evolve as well.

To summarize the findings: At 20 periods and 2 standard deviations you get containment between 88 and 89 percent in most markets. To keep that containment percentage constant when you shorten the calculation period to 10 days, you need to decrease the bandwidth from 2.0 to 1.9; and when you lengthen the calculation period to 50 days, you need to increase the bandwidth from 2.0 to 2.1.

For calculation periods less than 10 or greater than 50, changing the periodicity of the bars is more appropriate. For example, if you require a shorter calculation period than 10 days, a shift to hourly bars might be better than trying to squeeze the calculation period ever tighter. There are seven trading hours in an NYSE day; the first half hour from 9:30 a.m. to 10:00 a.m. should be counted as an hour. So 35 hours is equivalent to 5 days. As a general rule, try to keep the calculation period near 20 or 30, the ranges within which there is a lot of experience. That's better than trying to push the envelope and getting unexpected results.

Why a simple moving average? For years a father and son team advertised "better Bollinger Bands" in *Investor's Business Daily*. Their "secret"? They used an exponential moving average as the measure of central tendency. Yet this book still recommends a simple moving average. The reason is that a simple moving average is what is used in calculating the volatility used to set the bandwidth, so it is internally consistent to use the same average to set the center point. Can you use an exponential average? Of course. Any average will work. But in doing so you are introducing an extraneous factor that you might or might not have to pay attention to. In our testing, no clear advantage was conferred by using an exponential or front-weighted average, as you can see if you compare Figures 7.1 through 7.3. So in the absence of a compelling argument, you should stick to the simplest and most logical approach.

What about mismatching the calculation periods? One popular mismatch is using longer periods for volatility and shorter periods for the average. The idea is to capture information from the dominant volatility cycle for the bandwidth while using the best measure of trend for the midpoint—for example, using a 50-period moving average for the center point and a 20-period volatility for the bandwidth (Figure 7.4). This is done less than swapping the average types in our experience, but it is done. I frankly can't see why you would want to introduce yet another variable to an already complex process, but if it floats your boat...

One last variation that is quite popular is to deploy multiple bands at the same time. This can be done in two ways. One is to

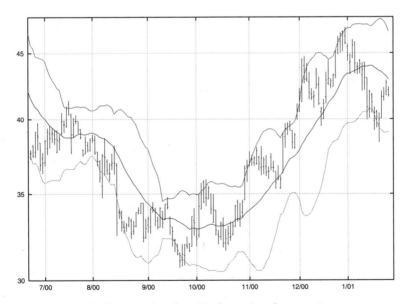

Figure 7.1 Bollinger Bands, 20-day simple moving average, Deere & Co., 150 days. Classic Bollinger Bands.

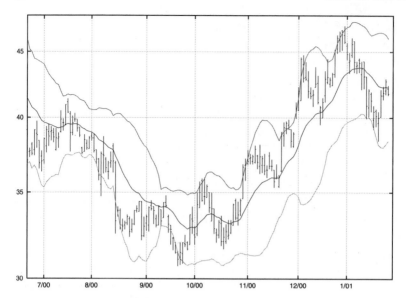

Figure 7.2   Bollinger Bands, 20-day exponential moving average, Deere & Co., 150 days. Exponential is faster—so you'd have to add periods to make it comparable.

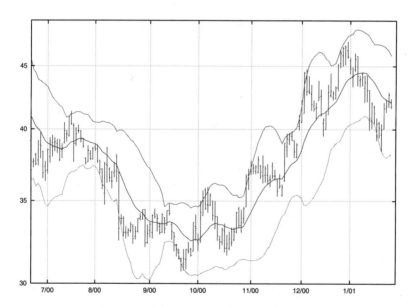

Figure 7.3   Bollinger Bands, 20-day front-weighted moving average, Deere & Co., 150 days. Front-weighted is even faster.

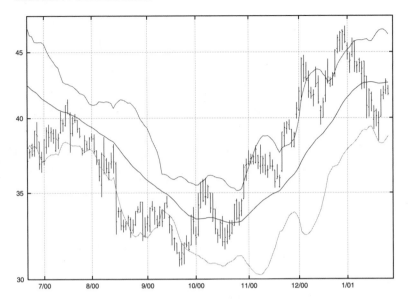

Figure 7.4 Bollinger Bands, 50-day moving average and 20-day standard deviation, Deere & Co., 150 days. Mix and match, or is that mix and mismatch?

plot multiple bands using the same calculation periods, say, 20 periods, but differing bandwidths, 1 and 2 standard deviations, for example (Figure 7.5). The other is to plot multiple sets of bands with different parameters, say, 20 periods and 2 standard deviations and 50 periods and 2.1 standard deviations, on the same chart (Figure 7.6). Of the two approaches, the most interesting is the latter. There are occasions where the disparate elements line up and mark interesting junctures. While this is not a recommended technique, it is a very interesting one and worth your attention after you have mastered the basics.

Life is complicated enough as it is. Stick to the basics and leave the wild stuff to those so inclined. After you have mastered the basic techniques, if you feel you can improve your performance by exploring the variations, feel free to do so. A solid foundation in pattern recognition (see Part III) and indicator use (see Part IV) will allow you to experiment and understand the pros and cons of the variations. So until you've got the basics down, try not to get lost in the woods.

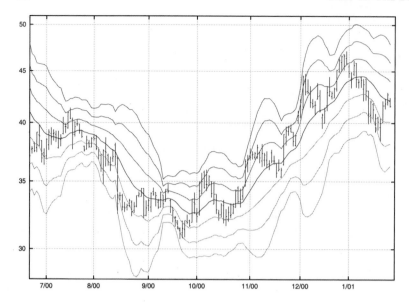

Figure 7.5 Multiple Bollinger Bands, equal periods, multiple widths, Deere & Co., 150 days. Aficionados claim that this presentation helps them see things better.

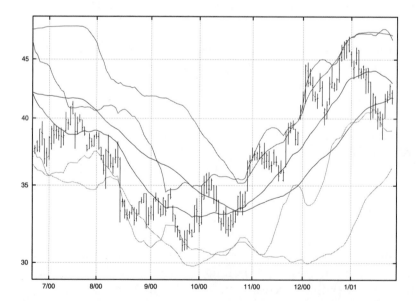

Figure 7.6 Multiple Bollinger Bands, different periods, normal widths, Deere & Co., 150 days. It's interesting to see where the bands come together.

KEY POINTS TO REMEMBER

- Use a simple moving average for the base.
- Use standard deviation to set the width.
- The defaults are 20 days and 2 standard deviations.
- Vary the bandwidth as a function of average length.
- Keep it simple.

8

BOLLINGER BAND INDICATORS

Two indicators can be derived directly from Bollinger Bands, %b and BandWidth. The first, %b, tells us where we are in relation to the Bollinger Bands and is the key to the development of trading systems via the linking of price and indicator action. The second, BandWidth, tells us how wide the bands are. BandWidth is the key to The Squeeze and can play an important role in spotting the beginnings and ends of trends. We'll tackle %b first and then BandWidth.

Table 8.1 shows the formula for %b. Note that the formula evaluates to 1.0 when the last price is at the upper band, 0.5 at the middle band, and 0.0 at the lower band. %b is not a bounded

Table 8.1 %b Formula[1]

(Last − lower BB)/(upper BB − lower BB)

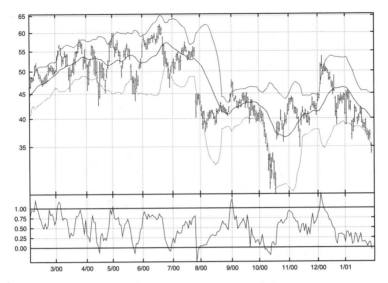

Figure 8.1   Bollinger Bands and %b, Nokia, 250 days. %b tells us where we are in relation to the bands.

formula. It will exceed 1 when the last price is above the upper band or will fall beneath zero when the last price is below the lower band. At 1.1 it says that we are 10 percent of the BandWidth above the upper band, and at −0.15 it says that we are 15 percent of the BandWidth below the lower band (Figure 8.1).

%b allows you to compare the price action within the Bollinger Bands with the action of an indicator, such as a volume oscillator (Figure 8.2). For example, suppose you decided on the following system: when price closes outside the upper Bollinger Band and the 21-day Intraday Intensity (II) is negative, sell. To program such a system, you might write: If %b is greater than one and 21-day II is less than zero, sell. More on this in Part IV.

Another important use of %b is to aid pattern recognition (Figure 8.3). For example, suppose you wanted to build a system that says if a retest of the lows is successful, then buy the first strong up day. To program that we might write: If %b at the first low is less than zero and %b at the second low is greater than zero, then buy the next up day if volume is greater than its 50-day average and range is greater than its 10-day average. More on this in Part III.

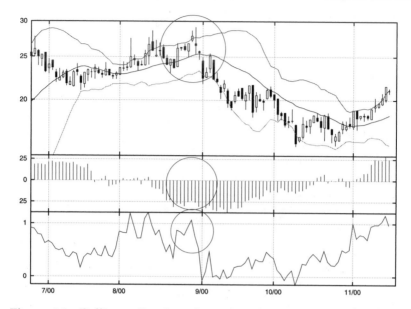

Figure 8.2 Bollinger Bands, %b, and 21-day Intraday Intensity, non-confirmed low, Guilford Pharmaceuticals, 100 days. Note the close above the upper band simultaneous with a negative indicator—a classic sell.

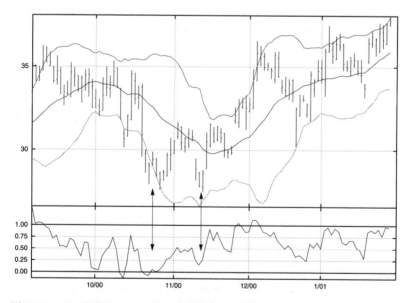

Figure 8.3 Bollinger Bands and %b, W bottom, Sears, 100 days. Note the W bottom with a new low in price but not for %b.

Table 8.2   BandWidth Formula

(Upper BB − lower BB)/middle BB

%b is a truly relative tool, spinning off no absolute information. It tells only where we are in relation to the framework created by the Bollinger Bands. It allows all sorts of relative comparisons. Take a situation in which you have plotted Bollinger Bands not only on price but also on an indicator and you wish to sell unconfirmed strength. You might write: If %b(price) is greater than 0.9 and %b(indicator) is less than 0.3, sell. But we are getting ahead of ourselves—this is discussed in the system presented in Chapter 20.

The second indicator derived from Bollinger Bands is BandWidth. To calculate BandWidth, subtract the lower band from the upper band and then normalize by dividing by the middle band, as shown in Table 8.2.[2] BandWidth can be calculated for any set of bands as long as they are based on a measure of central tendency such as a moving average.

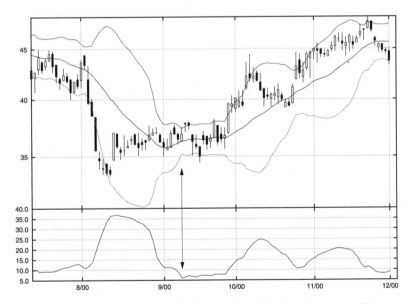

Figure 8.4   Bollinger Bands and BandWidth, The Squeeze, Clorox, 100 days. High volatility begets low volatility and vice versa.

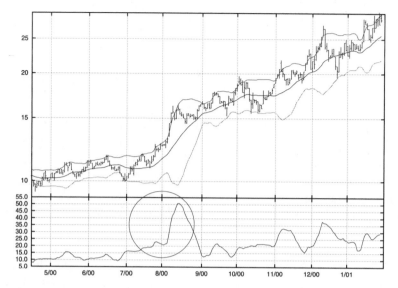

Figure 8.5 Bollinger Bands and BandWidth, beginning of a trend, Standard Pacific, 200 days. Note huge volatility pulse at the beginning of the trend.

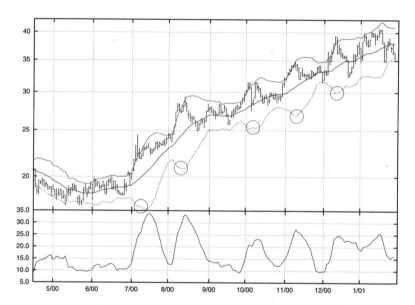

Figure 8.6 Bollinger Bands and BandWidth, end of a trend, Lennar, 200 days. Note that the opposite band turns up at the end of a leg up.

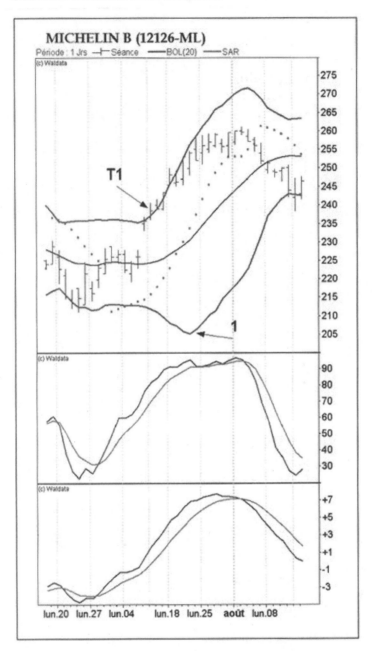

Figure 8.7 Steady volatility during a move. (SOURCE: "Paralleles" in *Analyse Technique Dynamique* by Philippe Cahen, Paris, France: Economica Books, 1999.)

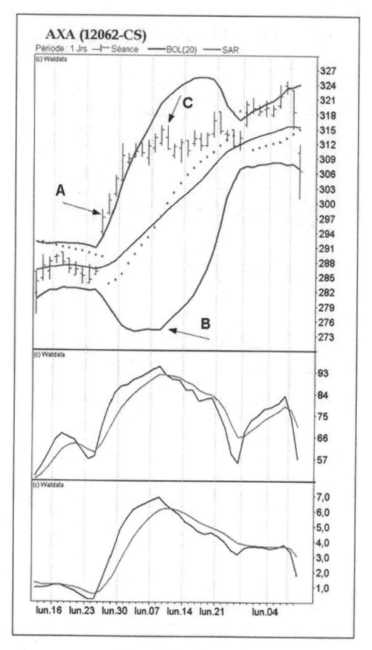

Figure 8.8 Variable volatility during a move. (SOURCE: "Bulle" in *Analyse Technique Dynamique* by Philippe Cahen, Paris, France: Economica Books, 1999.)

BandWidth is most useful for identifying The Squeeze, that situation where volatility has fallen to such a low level that its very lowness has become a forecast of increased volatility (Figure 8.4). The simplest approach to this is to note when BandWidth is at a six-month low. This is explored again in Chapter 15.

An important use of BandWidth is to mark the beginning of directional trends, either up or down. Many trends are born in trading ranges when the BandWidth is quite narrow. A breakout from the trading range that is accompanied by a sharp expansion in BandWidth is often the mark of the beginning of a sustainable trend (Figure 8.5).

Another important use of BandWidth is to mark the end of strong trends, themselves often born in Squeezes. What you'll see is that a strong trend will cause a large expansion in volatility that causes the bands to spread dramatically, so much so that the band on the other side of the trend—e.g., the lower band in an uptrend—will head in the direction opposite to the trend. *When that band reverses—turns back up in this case—that leg of the move is at an end.* This also can be seen and enumerated in BandWidth. The idea is when BandWidth flattens out or turns down enough to reverse the direction of the Bollinger Band on the opposite side of the trend, the trend is at an end (Figure 8.6).

Philippe Cahen, a French analyst, has written on the Bollinger Band patterns that are formed by changing BandWidth. Two patterns he refers to are "bubbles" and "parallels" (Figures 8.7 and 8.8). In each case he finds that volatility has a characteristic signature that, when depicted via Bollinger Bands, allows one to identify significant trading opportunities.[3]

KEY POINTS TO REMEMBER

- %b depicts where the last price is in relation to the bands.
- %b is useful in creating trading systems and signals.
- BandWidth depicts the width of the bands in a relative manner.
- BandWidth is used to identify The Squeeze.
- BandWidth is useful for identifying the beginnings and ends of trends.

9

STATISTICS

First, a bit of background:

Take a group of people and measure their heights. Now plot the number of people at each height (5′8″, 5′9″, etc.) on a bar chart. The result will be a normal distribution like that shown in Figure 9.1, a bell-shaped curve around the average height. Most of the people will be grouped around the average height forming the top of the bell. As you get away from the average, there will be ever-fewer people. By the time you get to the tall and short extremes, there will be just a few.

Conduct the same exercise with stock-price changes and you'll find that the tails, the extremes where the short and the tall were, are too thick. There are too many large gains and large losses, more than you would expect, and not enough small changes, less than you would expect. This means that stock prices are not normally

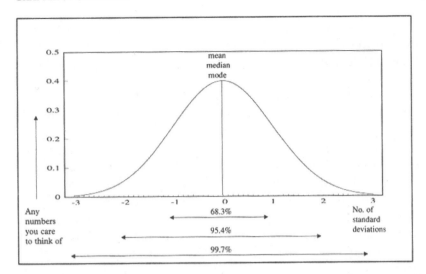

Figure 9.1 The normal distribution. (SOURCE: *The Economist Numbers Guide* by Richard Stutely, New York: John Wiley & Sons, 1998.)

distributed and the statistical rules you would normally expect to hold may not hold.

To get an accurate estimate of something, you may sample it. Take a bowl with a couple of hundred red and green marbles in it. If you pick 30 marbles at random from the bowl, the proportion of red to green in the sample you selected should reflect the proportion of the population—all the marbles in the bowl. The larger the sample, the better the reflection or estimate will be. If you have more than two colors, you'll need a larger sample size to get a good estimate.

Okay, if you can grasp that, the rest should be easy.

The use of standard deviation to drive the width of Bollinger Bands naturally invites the use (abuse?) of statistical rules. While many inferences are inappropriate due to the non-normal distribution of stock prices and the small sample sizes typically used, some statistical concepts do appear to hold.

The central limit theorem suggests that even when the data is not normally distributed—as is the case for stocks—a random sampling will produce a normally distributed subset for which the statistical rules will hold. This is thought to be true even at relatively small sample sizes. So we should not be surprised to learn that the statistical expectations do hold to some extent, even if everything isn't strictly kosher.

The statistical concept most often inquired about in relation to Bollinger Bands is regression to the mean, which says that all things will eventually come home; for statisticians home is the mean or average. Thus as prices depart from the average, we should expect them to move back toward the average. This is the statistical concept behind the technical terms *overbought* and *oversold*. Regression to the mean implies that prices at the edges of the distribution—at the upper or lower Bollinger Bands—will revert to the mean—the average, or middle, Bollinger Band.

While there is some evidence of regression to the mean demonstrated by financial instruments, it is not as strong as it should be, so *tags of the bands are not automatic buys or sells with the average as a target*. This is precisely why the use of indicators to confirm tags of the bands is such a powerful concept. With indicators we can make rational judgments about whether to expect regression to the mean or a continuation of the trend. When the chosen indicator confirms a tag of the bands, you do not have a buy or sell signal; you have a continuation signal. When a tag is unconfirmed, expect regression to the mean. In this manner we combine information from statistics with information from technical analysis, relying on the strengths of each to improve our decision making.

At sample sizes smaller than the minimum required for statistical significance, the basic statistical processes should still be relevant if the central limit theorem holds. Our testing confirms that this is the case for Bollinger Bands. While slight adjustments are desirable to maintain the proportion of data contained within the bands as the sample size changes (the number of days), the behavior exhibited in and around the bands is much the same whether the period is 10 days or 50 days. This is true even though only approximately 89 percent of the data is contained within 2 standard deviation bands when we would expect 95 percent.

There are two possible reasons why we don't get as high a level of containment as we would expect—near 95 percent with 2 standard deviation bands. First, we are using the population calculation, which results in slightly tighter bands than the sample calculation.[1] Second, the distribution of stock prices is not normal—there are more observations at the extremes than one would expect—so there are more data points outside the bands too. There are undoubtedly more factors, but these appear to be the main ones.

What is a non-normal distribution again? And what has a fat tail? The graph in Figure 9.2 illustrates the concept nicely. The taller hump is a normal distribution, the way things ought to be. The shorter hump is a distribution like the stock market's, less small changes than one would expect and more large changes. The amount of difference between the two humps is known as *kurtosis*, and it is a significant quantity for stocks.

Perhaps one of the most interesting aspects of Bollinger Bands is the rhythmic contraction and expansion of the bands you can see on the charts. This is especially clear in the bond market where a fairly regular 19-day volatility cycle can be observed (Figure 9.3). It turns out that there is a fair amount of academic research into this phenomenon. A search for papers on GARCH and ARCH^2 will reveal the details for those so inclined. In general, the idea is that while price is neither cyclical—in a regular sense—nor forecastable using cycles, volatility is both. So

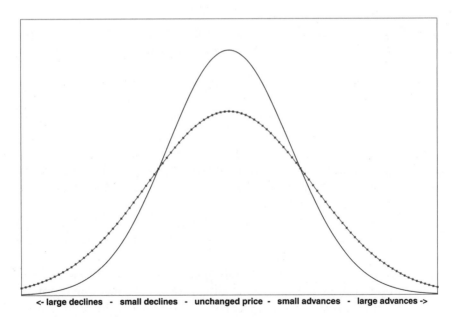

<- large declines - small declines - unchanged price - small advances - large advances ->

Figure 9.2 Kurtosis. The stock market is not normally distributed—too many large changes.

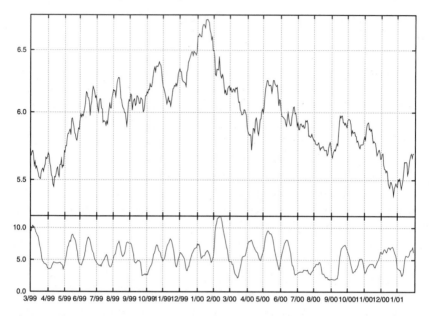

Figure 9.3 Bond market volatility cycle, 30-year T-bond yield, two years. Note the regular distance between the lows in volatility.

we should not be surprised to see a regular pattern to the expansion and contraction of the bands as they reflect volatility about an average, even if such a cycle is not detectable in price. The word *regular* is the trap. While the volatility cycle of long-term interest rates does seem to have a fairly regular 19-day interval, the volatility cycles exhibited for most other financial instruments are nowhere near as regular. However, it is not the regularity or lack thereof that is interesting. The most interesting conclusion is that low volatility begets high volatility and high volatility begets low volatility. This is the foundation of The Squeeze (see Chapter 15).

The bottom line is that while the rules relating to the statistical nature of the Bollinger Bands hold in a general manner, we can make few assertions based on the statistical validity of the calculations used to compute Bollinger Bands. Clearly stocks are not widgets on a manufacturing line, and trying to treat them as such is foolhardy. Just as clearly, a great deal of effort and creativity has gone into statistics, and there are statistical tools available that can be adapted to the needs of investing.

KEY POINTS TO REMEMBER

- Statistical rules hold generally, but not absolutely, for Bollinger Bands.
- Regression to the mean is not as strong as it should be.
- Use indicators to confirm band tags.
- Volatility is cyclical even when price is not.
- High volatility begets low, and low volatility begets high.

PART III

BOLLINGER BANDS ON THEIR OWN

Part III delves into the most basic function of technical analysis, pattern recognition, and demonstrates how Bollinger Bands can be used to aid successful pattern recognition. Tops, bottoms, and sustained trends each have their own chapter. Finally, you will find the first of the three trading methods—this one based on The Squeeze.

10

PATTERN
RECOGNITION

Pattern recognition refers to the process by which we recognize recurring events. Typically such events have a signature consisting of a number of discrete pieces that, when combined in specific sequences, allow us to recognize the pattern and act upon it. These patterns rarely, if ever, repeat exactly. Rather, they are only generally the same, and there lies the rub. In order to be successful at pattern recognition, we need some framework within which these patterns can be analyzed, and Bollinger Bands can provide that framework.

The literature of technical analysis is rife with descriptions of technical patterns. Double bottoms and tops, head-and-shoulders formations (regular and inverted), and ascending and descending triangles are but a few of the more common patterns. Some patterns imply trend reversals, and others are continuation patterns.[1]

Bollinger Bands can aid in pattern recognition by providing definitions: high and low, calm or volatile, trending or not— definitions that can be compared from time to time, from issue to issue, and from market to market. As the patterns evolve, the bands evolve right along with them, providing a relative, flexible framework rather than the absolute, rigid framework imposed by the grid of a chart or the hardness of a trend line.

Securities rarely transition from bullish phases to bearish phases or vice versa in an abrupt manner. The transitions usually involve a sequence of price action that typically includes one or more tests of support or resistance. Ms and Ws are examples of patterns that form at turning points in the markets and let us know that the prior trend has ended and a new trend has started. That new trend can be a reversal of a prior uptrend or downtrend, a transition from a trendless state, or it could be the beginning of a sideways trend such as a consolidation. Most common are double bottoms and head-and-shoulders tops. But not all reversal patterns are W bottoms or extended M tops characterized by three "pushes"; they are merely the most common (Figures 10.1 and 10.2).

Spike tops and V bottoms can and do occur, marking virtually instantaneous transitions from up to down or vice versa. Some reversal patterns don't turn out to be reversal patterns at all; they simply mark the end of the prior trend and a transition to a sideways market, rather than the beginning of a new trend in the opposite direction. Then there are longer, more complex patterns too: gradual transitions from downtrends to uptrends known as bases, congestion patterns, and complex tops.

Often patterns are small parts of larger patterns that can be seen only on a longer scale, say, by shifting from an hourly view to a daily view, or from a weekly view to a monthly view. There was a trading system[2] created in the late 1980s that used three time frames and required that the patterns or signals be similar in all three time frames before a trade was taken. This was a "fractal"[3] approach to the markets and one of the most eloquent demonstrations of the importance of overlapping time frames ever presented.

It turns out that fractal patterns are very common. For example, take a long-term W bottom. When examined closely, the W may turn out to have intermediate-term W bottoms

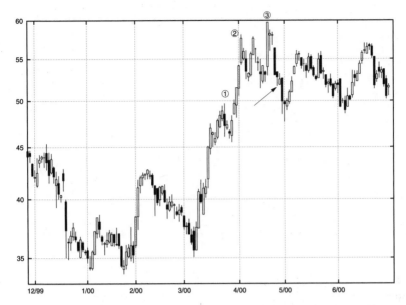

Figure 10.1 Three pushes to a high, Pharmacia, 150 days. Three pushes to a high followed by sharp downside action that breaks the trend.

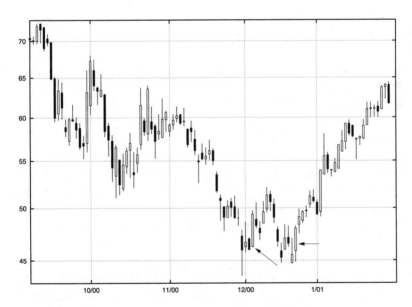

Figure 10.2 W bottom, Bear Sterns, 100 days. Classic W bottom—note the positive candlesticks right after the lows.

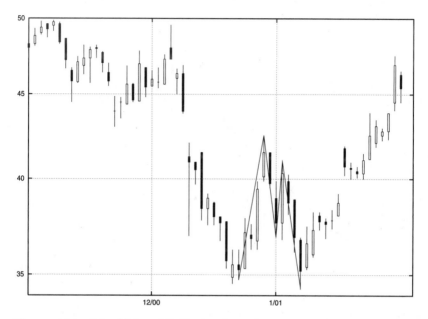

Figure 10.3   M within a W, Harley Davidson, 100 days. Can you see the M within the W?

embedded in its footings; and often you'll see a small M formation appear at the apex of the W (Figure 10.3). There is really no limit to this fractal quality, though more than two or three levels are rarely observed at work concurrently.

Regardless of the level of magnification, technical patterns refer to a sequence of price action that forms a typical pattern on the chart with a recognizable signature—a pattern and signature that can be elucidated with Bollinger Bands. To wit:

An ideal example of a W (a double bottom) involves an initial decline followed by a recovery rally, and then a secondary decline followed in turn by the initiation of an uptrend. It isn't important whether the second decline makes a new low or not—at least in absolute terms. The first low will be outside the lower Bollinger Band, while the second low will fall inside it. Volume will be higher on the first decline than on the second (Figure 10.4).

A similar top is not necessarily a perfect mirror of the bottom's pattern; the top will likely take more time and consist of three (or more) upward thrusts to complete the pattern rather than just

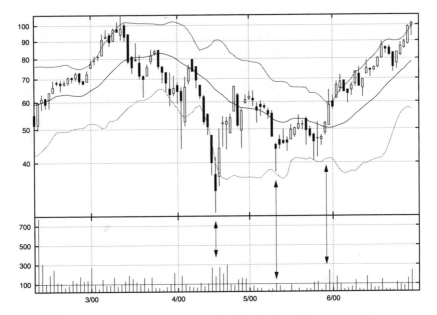

Figure 10.4 W bottom, Bollinger Bands, and volume confirmation, Art Technology Group, 100 days. Strong volume on the first low, weak volume on the second low, and strong volume on the liftoff.

two. Such a top will likely be a variation on the head-and-shoulders pattern.

Bollinger Bands can dramatically clarify the patterns you see on the charts. An ideal W is a momentum low that occurs outside the lower Bollinger Band, followed by a price low inside the lower band. Even if the final price low has driven to a new absolute low, *it is not a new low on a relative basis.* Therefore the ensuing rally can be acted upon without the emotion usually coincident with a new low in price.

To help categorize these patterns, you should think of momentum highs and lows followed by price highs and lows. Typically in a decline you'll get an accelerated move into the first low; this is where the momentum is the highest, a fact that is usually confirmed by very high volume. Then will come a period of recovery followed by a decline that will establish the price low, which may well be a new low in price but which will occur with greatly reduced momentum and volume. In many cases the momentum peaks and troughs will occur outside the Bollinger Bands and the subsequent price peaks and troughs will occur inside the Bollinger Bands.

Another way of thinking about tops and bottoms is as processes that consume momentum. So in addition to the volume indicators that we favor in this book, momentum indicators can be very useful in the diagnostic process. A useful analytical approach is to plot both a volume indicator and a momentum indicator (Figure 10.5). Each operates independently of the other, so when they signal together, they afford a high level of confidence in the outlook for the stock.

Although one of the most important uses of Bollinger Bands is in diagnosing tops and bottoms, there are other important pattern-recognition uses: identifying continuing trends, defining trading ranges, and recognizing The Squeeze.

Pattern recognition is the key to successful technical investing. And Bollinger Bands, especially when coupled with indicators, are the key to successful pattern recognition. The next chapter

Figure 10.5 W bottom, Bollinger Bands, volume indicator, and momentum indicator, Art Technology Group, 100 days. Less downside momentum and less volume on the retest.

presents a method of categorizing patterns that will stand you in good stead in all market conditions.

KEY POINTS TO REMEMBER

- Ms and Ws are the most common patterns.
- Patterns are often fractal.
- Bollinger Bands can be used to clarify patterns.
- Lows (highs) outside the bands followed by lows (highs) inside the bands are typically reversal patterns even if a new absolute low or high is made.
- Volume and momentum indicators are very useful for diagnosing tops and bottoms.

11

FIVE-POINT
PATTERNS

Virtually all stock-price patterns can be neatly classified with the aid of a simple tool, the price filter. This approach connects high and low points on a chart where the swings between the points exceed a certain number of points or, more usefully, a certain percentage.

A useful point filter might be as large as 100 points for the Dow Jones Industrial Average, or as small as 2 points for IBM. As the price levels change, these fixed-point amounts represent different percentage values. It is generally better to employ a percentage filter that has the same economic value at all price levels. Certainly for stocks, point filters really aren't worth considering.[1] An 8 percent filter would amount to $\frac{8}{10}$ of a point at 10, but 8 points at 100, whereas an 8-point filter would be 8 percent at 100 and 80 percent at 10. These results are highly variable due to the wide range of prices at which stocks trade, thus point filters are not comparable from issue to issue.

Percentage filters between 2 and 10 percent usually work well for stocks and offer comparability from issue to issue. Figures 11.1 through 11.6 illustrate the percentage filter in action. Each chart depicts the same series, but employs a successively higher percentage price filter. The resulting zigzag lines eliminate an ever-greater amount of noise, until we reach the final example— Figure 11.6—where the entire chart is characterized by a single swing. The goal of these swing charts is to filter price sufficiently to clarify the patterns without eliminating important information.

Another filtering method similar to zigzags or swing charts is point and figure. Point-and-figure charts, which may be the oldest Western stock charting method, are based purely on price swings, which are recorded without reference to time or volume. Point-and-figure charts are kept on square-ruled graph paper, and each individual portion of the grid is referred to as a box. Price levels are marked at the left, on the y axis.

Point-and-figure charts appear in the literature as early as the late 1800s, with references to "figure charts" being kept on the

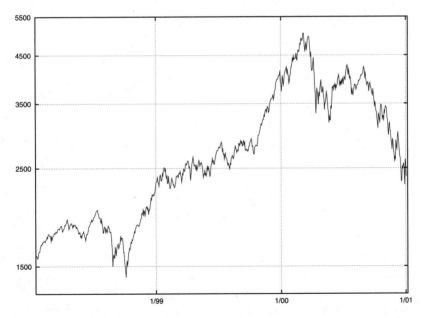

Figure 11.1 NASDAQ Composite, three years, no filter. The raw data.

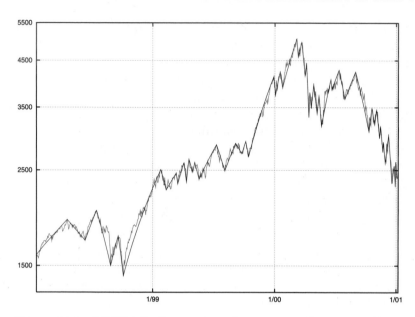

Figure 11.2 NASDAQ Composite, three years, 5 percent filter. The filter starts to clean things up.

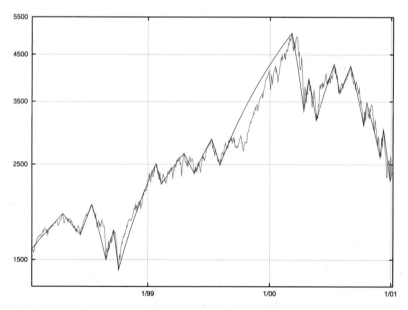

Figure 11.3 NASDAQ Composite, three years, 10 percent filter. Shows a pretty good picture of the important swings.

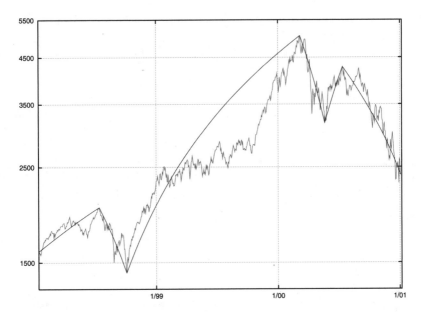

Figure 11.4 NASDAQ Composite, three years, 20 percent filter. Too filtered—important detail is being lost.

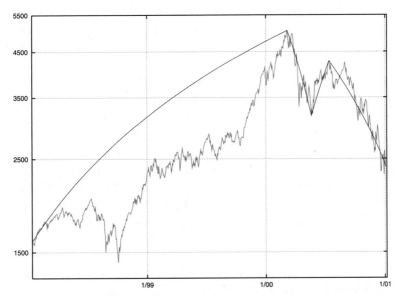

Figure 11.5 NASDAQ Composite, three years, 30 percent filter. Shows just the really big picture. (Filter lines curved due to log scaling.)

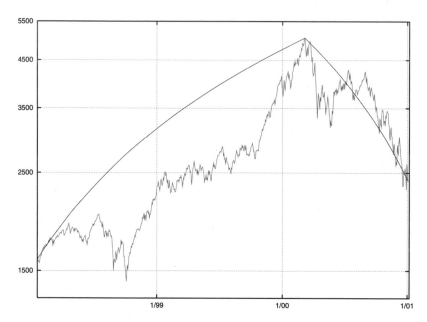

Figure 11.6 NASDAQ Composite, three years, 40 percent filter. This is way too filtered; no signal left.

exchange floor. Today they are marked with Xs for upswings and Os for downswings. The original "figure" charts are thought to have used the actual figures—3, 21, 57, etc.—in the boxes to record price action. Floor traders wrote them by hand on the backs of trade tickets. Then came point-and-figure charts composed with Xs plotted in both directions, but with 0s and 5s when the price ended in 0 or 5; deVilliers and Wheelan, published analysts, both used this method (Figure 11.7).

The modern process of keeping a point-and-figure chart is fairly simple, and the charts can be kept easily by hand (Figure 11.8). Xs are placed successively higher in a column of boxes as price rises; then as price falls, Os are placed in the next column to the right. The transition from a rising column of Xs to a falling column of Os is triggered by a reversal that exceeds a predetermined limit, usually a number of boxes, most often three. The opposite is true for a transition from Os to Xs.

Point-and-figure practitioners have long faced the problem of selecting an appropriate filter or box value. They generally use a rule based on the price of the stock. At low price levels each box

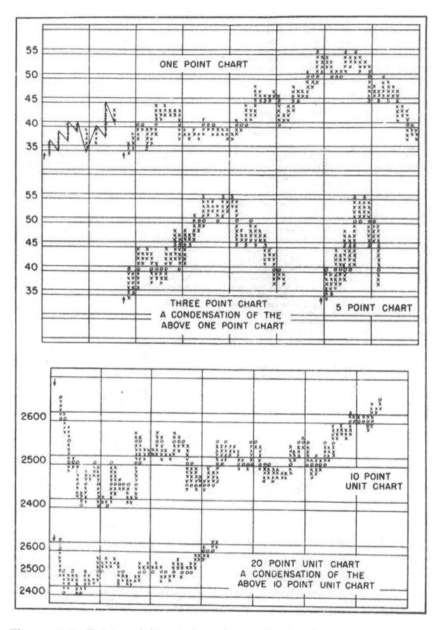

Figure 11.7   Point-and-figure chart from Wheelan. [SOURCE: *Study Helps in Point and Figure Technique* by Alexander H. Wheelan, originally published by Morgan, Rogers, and Roberts (New York, 1947), reprinted by Fraser Publishing (Burlington, Vt., 1989).]

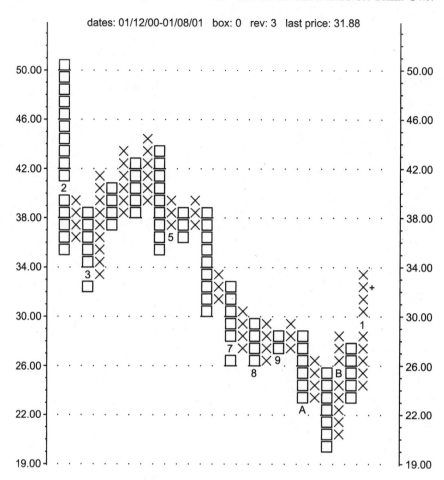

Figure 11.8   Modern point-and-figure chart, IBM, one year.

might represent a quarter point or a half point. At higher prices the box size is increased so that each square on the grid, or box, might now denote a half point or a full point. For a $10 stock each box might be a point, or for an $80 stock each box might represent a point and a half. The ChartCraft approach, originally developed by Abe Cohen, is the most widely accepted. Table 11.1 presents the ChartCraft box-size recommendations.

   In order to switch from a negative swing to a positive swing, using the ChartCraft system, a three-box threshold is employed. This allows for a small enough box size that vital detail is not lost

Table 11.1 ChartCraft Recommended Box Sizes for Stocks

Price Range	Box Size
Below $5	¼ point
Between $5 and $20	½ point
Between $20 and $100	1 point
Above $100	2 points

at the same time a large enough filter is employed. So with the ChartCraft method, for a $10 stock a 1½-point reversal is needed to change swing direction ½ * 3. For a $70 stock a 6-point reversal is required to change swing direction (2 * 3).

The main problem with this approach is variability—abrupt, large changes at transition prices. For example, a $19 stock, with its half-point boxes, reverses swings with a 1½-point move, whereas a $20 stock, with its full-point boxes, requires a 3-point swing to reverse. Normally reversals get smaller in percentage terms as price rises, but there are places where higher prices beget higher percentage reversal values due to transitions in box sizes. Using our example, a $19 stock uses a 7.8 percent reversal, whereas a $20 stock uses a 15 percent reversal. You have to rally all the way to $40 before you get back to a 7.5 percent reversal.

A simple method of *smoothly specifying box size*, Bollinger Boxes, was developed in order to avoid the problems caused by the traditional rules. To create Bollinger Boxes, all of the historical methods used to specify box size from Wheelan to Cohen were tabulated. Then the rule sets were plotted, with price on the x axis and percent box size on the y axis. For each set of rules this process produced a stepped line to which a curve was fit (Figure 11.9). The formula for that curve was noted and the procedure repeated for each known box-size methodology. These procedures revealed an ideal box size that can be simplified to 17 percent of the square root of the most recent price (see Table 11.2).

As a control, the square root rule (SRR) was used. The earliest mention of the SRR is in Burton Crane's 1959 book, *The Sophisticated Investor*, where he cites Fred Macauley's writings in the *New York Times-Annalist* magazine as the original source.[2] The SRR suggests that volatility is a function of the square root of price;

Table 11.2 Sample Box Sizes Using Simplified Bollinger Boxes $(0.17 * last^{0.5})$

Price	Reversal
$4.5	8%
$8	6%
$18	4%
$69	2%

for an equal move in the market, stocks will rally such that the square roots of their initial prices change by a similar amount. This rule produces large percentage gains for low-priced issues and large point gains for high-priced issues. From this perspective, low-price stocks are more volatile than high-price stocks. This is an intuitively correct idea. On average we expect that low-price stocks will experience greater percentage increases and decreases than high-price stocks.

There was relatively little variation between the historical methods that were plotted, and the fits to the SRR were near perfect.

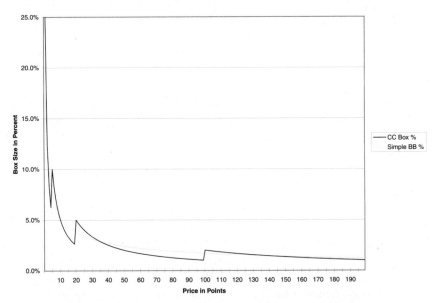

Figure 11.9 Curve fit for Cohen's point-and-figure box-size rules.

Using Bollinger Boxes to construct point-and-figure charts frees one from the artificial barriers created by the boundaries where box size is changed. This is obviously easier to do by computer, but then almost all technical analysis is computerized these days.[3]

Having developed an ideal approach to filtering stock prices, we may now proceed to categorizing the arising patterns. The first attempt to systematically categorize price patterns was made in 1971 by Robert Levy. He used five-point patterns delineated by price swings governed by each stock's volatility in his categorization and then tested those patterns for significance. Though he was unable to discover any significant forecasting power,[4] he left behind a powerful tool, the five-point categorization.

This approach lay dormant for 10 years until Arthur A. Merrill picked it up and published positive results in the early 1980s. He used the same five-point approach, but used an 8 percent filter instead of Levy's volatility filter. He ordered the patterns into two groups, 16 patterns with the general shape of a capital M and 16 with the general shape of a capital W.[5]

Merrill categorized the patterns by the sequential order of the points from high to low, creating an orderly taxonomy of Ms and Ws. An M1 is a strongly falling pattern, the middle patterns M8 and M9 are flat patterns, and an M16 is a strongly rising pattern (Figure 11.10). Likewise a W1 is a falling pattern, the middle Ws are flat, and a W16 is a rising pattern (Figure 11.11).

You also will find these patterns on the inside of the reference card bound into the back of this book. Merrill went on to show that some of these patterns had forecasting implications on their own. See his book *M&W Wave Patterns* for further information. Merrill also categorized some of the patterns according to the traditional names used by market technicians (see Table 11.3).

Where Merrill used a fixed-percentage filter, Levy used volatility to filter the patterns. We favor a combination of the two, Bollinger Boxes for filtering the swings and volatility for projecting the subsequent moves. Indeed, this approach lies at the core of our institutional trading platform, PatternPower, www.PatternPower.com.

One important aspect of M and W patterns is that they can be clarified using Bollinger Bands and indicators. In the following two chapters (Chapters 12 and 13) we'll consider Ms and Ws

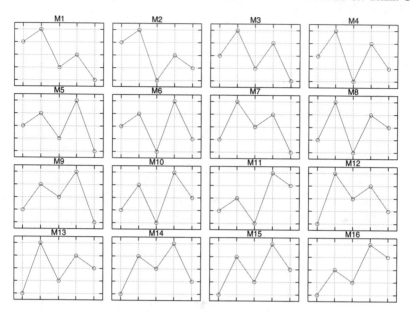

Figure 11.10 Arthur Merrill's M patterns. (SOURCE: *M & W Wave Patterns* by Arthur A. Merrill, Chappaqua, N.Y.: Analysis Press, 1983.)

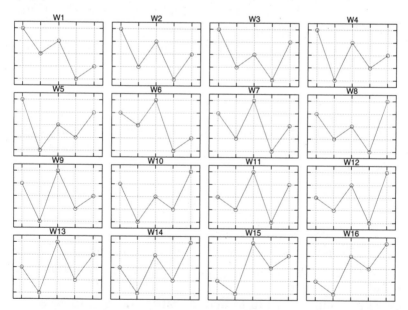

Figure 11.11 Arthur Merrill's W patterns. (SOURCE: *M & W Wave Patterns* by Arthur A. Merrill, Chappaqua, N.Y.: Analysis Press, 1983.)

Table 11.3 Merrill's Categorization of M and W Patterns

Technical Patterns	Merrill's Patterns
Uptrends	M15, M16, W14, W16
Downtrends	M1, M3, W1, W2
Head and shoulders	W6, W7, W9, W11, W13, W15
Inverted head and shoulders	M2, M4, M6, M8, M10, M11
Triangle	M13, W4
Broadening	M5, W12

separately, as they are quite different in character, and show you how to combine them with Bollinger Bands to increase your forecasting accuracy. Finally in Chapter 14 we'll add indicators to the mix.

KEY POINTS TO REMEMBER

- Price filters can be used to filter out noise and clarify patterns.
- Percentage filters are best for stocks.
- Bollinger Boxes offer a superior filtering approach.
- All price patterns can be categorized as a series of Ms and Ws.

12

W-TYPE BOTTOMS

From here on out we'll be using M and W patterns to describe what's going on with price action. All the patterns are laid out on two pages of your reference card (which is bound into the back of the book), Ms on the left and Ws on the right. Pull it out (if you haven't already done so) so you can consult it easily when you need to.

We'll start with bottom formations. They are generally cleaner, clearer, and easier to diagnose than top formations. The difference lies in the underlying psychology; bottoms are created in an environment of fear and pain, quite different from the environment of euphoria and hope in which tops are formed.[1] Thus we expect bottoms to be sharper and more tightly focused, to take less time and be more dramatic. Pain is, after all, a more insistent emotion than joy. Likewise we expect tops to be more prolonged affairs, typically more diffuse and harder to diagnose. Investors simply do not feel the need to act at tops in the same urgent manner they do at bottoms.

In the process of researching a recent project, we tested the characteristics of price patterns at intermediate lows and highs. Double bottoms and triple tops were the rule, and the time spent forming tops was greater than that spent in bottoms. This confirmed Wall Street lore that "down is faster" and agrees with what one would expect from a psychological perspective.[2]

Stocks rarely transition from a declining phase to an advancing phase in a crisp manner. Rather, they most often recover a bit, fall back to test support, and then rally. The pattern this process creates is called a double, or W, bottom (see Figure 12.1). The W is the most common bullish transition type, but it is not the only one. Though they are relatively rare, there are examples of stocks that plunge to new lows, turn on a dime, and rocket away. A stock making a V bottom may have stumbled across unexpected good fortune, or good news may suddenly be released, breaking the downtrend and instantly reversing the stock's fortunes. More common is the stock that falls to a new low, then trades sideways for a long time, then turns higher—"base building" in the parlance. This is often a stock that has had fundamental problems

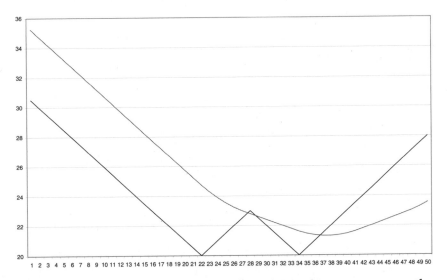

Figure 12.1 The ideal W, drawing. Typical W—the average stops the first rally but not the second.

and needs time to get its house in order. However, most frequent
of all is the W bottom, a low followed by a retest and then an
uptrend. This is typical of a stock completing a correction where
the stream of fundamental facts about the company is not in
question, where the questions are relatively minor, or where the
questions are resolved in favor of the company before serious
damage is done.

Ws can be formed in any number of ways, each with their own
emotional color. The right-hand side of the formation can be
higher than (Figure 12.2), equal to (Figure 12.3), or lower than
(Figure 12.4) the left side. Each can be categorized as a Merrill
pattern, and each depicts a distinct psychological pattern. Where
the right side of the W is higher, frustration is the main emotion
when investors waiting for a "proper retest" are left standing at
the door as the stock rallies away from them. W4, W5, and W10
patterns are good examples of this. When the lows on the left
and right sides of the formation are equal, satisfaction is the
main emotion as investors buy into the retest without much
trouble and are rewarded quickly. When the low on the right-hand

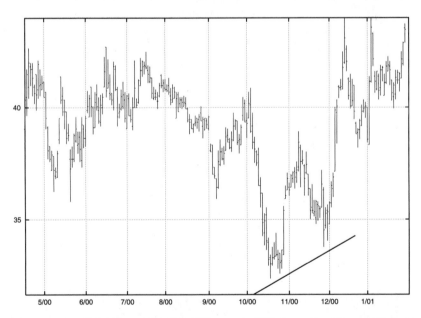

Figure 12.2   W higher, New York Times A, 200 days. Retest at a higher
level.

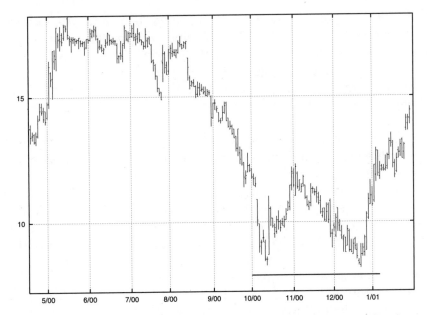

Figure 12.3   W equal, JCPenney, 200 days. Retest at the same level.

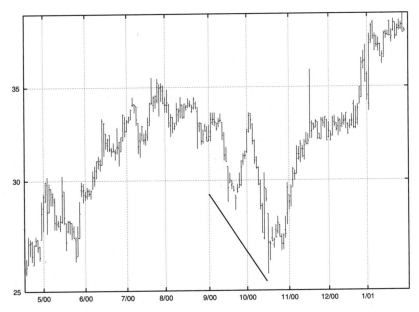

Figure 12.4   W lower, Starwood Hotels, 200 days. Retest at a lower level.

side of the formation is a lower low, fear and discomfort characterize the crowd. W2, W3, and W8 patterns are good examples. Investors who bought at the prior low are shaken out, and few have the courage necessary to get back in; at the same time new money is scared away by the lower low. In Wyckoff (referring to technical analyst Richard D. Wyckoff) terms this is called a spring.

Usually the left-hand side of a W formation—the first low, that is—will either be in contact with the lower band or be outside the lower band (Figure 12.5). The reaction rally will carry price back inside our bands, often tagging or exceeding the middle band in doing so. Then, the subsequent retest will occur inside the lower Bollinger Band. Remember, our definition of low is the lower Bollinger Band. So if the first low occurs outside the band and the second low occurs inside the band, *the second low is higher on a relative basis even if it is lower on an absolute basis.* An absolute W8 may turn out to be a relative W10, a much easier formation to deal with. Thus the Bollinger Bands can help you diagnose and act on

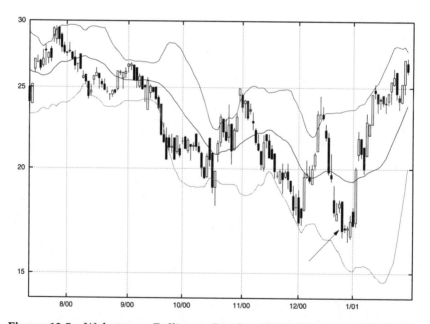

Figure 12.5 W bottom, Bollinger Bands, AT&T Wireless, 140 days. A new absolute low, but not a new relative low.

the trickiest of formations, the shakeout, where the potential for gains is great.

There will be examples of secondary lows occurring at or beneath the lower band and/or making new relative lows (Figure 12.6). These do not fit our categorization and are not, for our purposes at least, valid W bottoms. Please reread Chapter 4, "Continuous Advice," at this time if the concept of an undiagnosable formation rubs you the wrong way.

A stock does not have to trade beneath the lower band at the first low for a classic W bottom to be valid (Figure 12.7). All that is really called for is that price be relatively higher on the second retest. This requirement can be satisfied by price nearing, but not touching, the lower band on the initial pass, then trading only halfway between the lower band and the middle band on the retest. %b is very helpful in this regard, as will be discussed later.

Often bottom formations such as the double bottom, or W, contain smaller formations within them, especially at the next higher level of magnification. So if you are examining a bottom

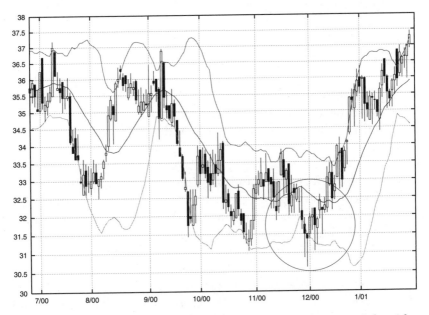

Figure 12.6 W bottom, lower Bollinger Band broken on right side, Ashland, 150 days. The excursion outside the lower band breaks the rules.

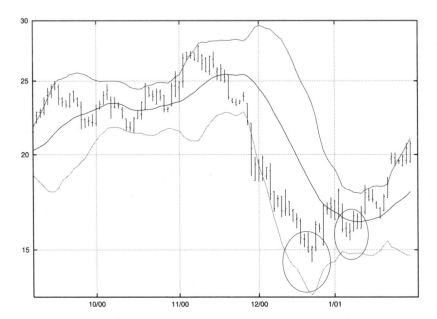

Figure 12.7 W bottom, neither low breaks the bands, The Limited, 100 days. A W completely inside the bands.

pattern forming on the daily chart, look for small-scale patterns on the hourly charts confirming the turns in the larger pattern developing on the daily charts.

Okay, so now you have found a W that fits the rules and that you are comfortable with—what do you do? Buy strength. Wait for a rally day with greater than average range and greater than average volume and buy (Figure 12.8). This day confirms your diagnosis of the formation and sets the stage for the rally.

Your stop should go beneath the most recent low—the right side of the W—and should be incremented upward as soon as is reasonable. Either you may use an approach similar to the Welles Wilders Parabolic System that increments the stop each day, or you may increment by eye, setting the stop a bit beneath the lowest point of the most recent consolidation or pullback.

The room which you give prices to fluctuate by setting your stops will greatly impact your performance. Stops that are set too tight will result in too many broken trades, while stops that are too loose will allow too great a portion of your profits to be retraced.

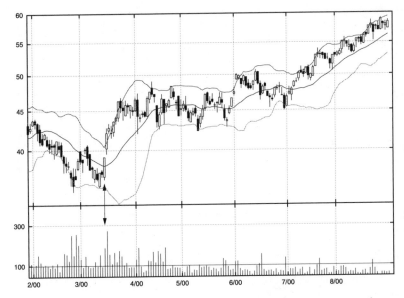

Figure 12.8 W bottom, buy the expansion day, Chevron, 150 days. A surge in volume plus a large positive daily range after a W is a buy signal.

The best advice is to start with relatively wide stops and tighten them slowly until the risk-reward trade-offs suit your style.

In categorizing lows we find that the formations often have similar fundamental and psychological factors. In this we are reminded of our goal and indeed the purpose of technical analysis: to identify junctures in the market where the odds favor the assumption of a position. In order for this to be true, we must be able to believe in the patterns we are seeing, and in order to believe, we must understand the factors that lead to the formation. Technical analysis is not a stand-alone science; rather it is a depiction of the actions of investors driven by fundamental and psychological facts—or more properly, driven by anticipation of the facts.

The argot of technical analysis is rife with terms that describe various setups, some sharply, some vaguely, and some incomprehensively. It is only to the extent that such terms successfully model underlying realities that they are useful. For example, a W bottom with a lower right-hand side often becomes an inverted

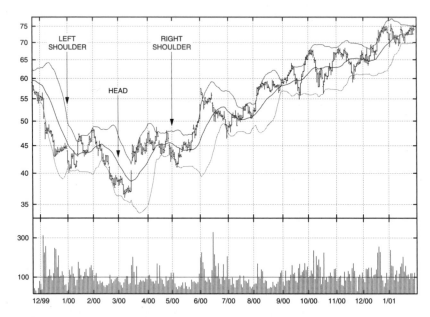

Figure 12.9 Head and shoulders, W8 and W10, PNC, 300 days. A complex W may be a head-and-shoulders formation.

head-and-shoulders pattern (see Figure 12.9) when a final retest of support occurs after the uptrend has been born—a W8 becomes a W14 or W16 after another two more price swings. Simply put, the nascent uptrend is met with skepticism and profit taking, creating a decline that forms the right shoulder. However, head-and-shoulders formations fit more properly in the domain of top formations, which is what we cover next.

KEY POINTS TO REMEMBER

- W bottoms and their variations are the most common.
- Spike bottoms do happen, but they are rare.
- Ws may be transitions to bases rather than reversals.
- Bollinger Bands can help clarify Ws.
- Buy strength after the completion of a W.
- Set a trailing stop to control risk.
- Potential W bottoms are listed each trading day on www.BollingeronBollingerBands.com.

13

M-TYPE TOPS

Tops are quite different from bottoms, and Ms are different from Ws. Speed, volatility, volume, and definition—all are apt to be different. Thus tops and bottoms of similar importance will not necessarily be mirrors of one another. Their patterns are a function of psychology. Panic is a much sharper, more forceful emotion than greed, so panic's portrayal on the chart is much clearer. Where the most typical bottoming pattern is a double bottom, or W, tops are typically more complex, with the most typical formation being the triple top. Just as in the case of panic bottoms, cases of spike tops do occur where an uptrend is sharply reversed, but they are relatively rare. Far more common are M-type tops, or double tops, that consist of a rally, a pullback, a subsequent failed test of resistance in the neighborhood of the prior highs, followed by the start of a downtrend. Most common of all, however, is the triple top, and a common variation of this is the head-and-shoulders top (this is perhaps the technical term recognized by the widest range of investors).

The head-and-shoulders pattern (see Figure 13.1) consists of a rally followed by a shallow pullback that forms the left shoulder. Then the head is formed by a rally to a new high followed by a steeper pullback that typically ends near the low established by the first pullback. An M15 pattern would be typical of this phase. Finally a failure rally that is unable to make a new high—ideally ending near the first peak—followed by a decline that falls beneath the levels established by the first and second declines—a level known as the neckline—forms the right shoulder. The new pattern could be the M15 morphing into an M12 or M7 after two more price swings. The last part of the formation is a throwback rally, which carries prices back into the neighborhood of the neckline. After the final two swings, we now have an M1 or M3 pattern. From there the decline begins in earnest. Volume in a head-and-shoulders rally also has a typical pattern—strongest on the left side of the formation, waning across the middle, and picking up as the decline gets under way.

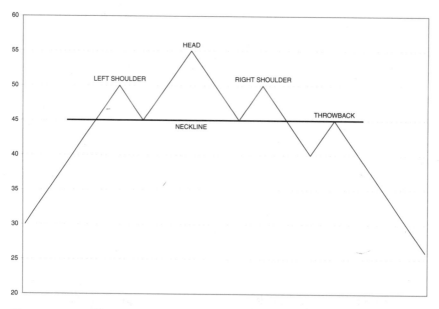

Figure 13.1 Idealized head-and-shoulders top. The most commonly known chart pattern.

Both the price pattern and the accompanying volume are closely linked to the underlying psychology. Euphoria and greed characterize the left side of the formation, with rumor often the dominant informational vehicle. Volume is high and activity heavy. The head is often accompanied by the release of the news that the rumors anticipated. Although we are at a new high, volume does not confirm. Here the old saw "sell on the news" comes into play, as those who bought in anticipation of the news, or due to the rumor, move to take profits. Their selling, accompanied by some short selling by the pessimists, forms the right side of the head and sets the stage for a last, weak bout of optimism that forms the right shoulder. Action is desultory and volume low. Now the decline sets in for real, the neckline is broken, and volume picks up again and fear surges. Finally, the covering of short sales by those who anticipated the decline and sold short near the highs is often said to be a factor in the throwback rally to the neckline. (Short sellers have to buy their shares back to close their positions.) The throwback rally is the last good chance to get out; ahead lie lower prices. See Figure 13.2 for a real-world example.

Fortunately, the diagnosis of all this is greatly helped by Bollinger Bands. The easiest way to tackle tops is to break them down into their component parts and treat them as a series of Ms and Ws. These smaller pattern components are much easier to cope with than the big pattern, but first let's look at the big pattern in an ideal sense.

The classic pattern would be a left shoulder outside the upper Bollinger Band, a head that tagged the upper band, and a right shoulder that failed well short of the upper band (Figure 13.3). In an ideal world the neckline would coincide with the middle band at the right shoulder, and the first decline would stop at the lower band. The throwback rally would stop at the middle band, and, finally, dramatically, the first leg down would break the lower band. That's the ideal, but the odds of seeing such a pattern, perfect in every respect, are not high. Much more common would be a pattern that obeyed most of those rules, offering general guidance as the pattern unfolded.

There is one very common variation of the head-and-shoulders pattern you should be aware of, three pushes to a high (Figure 13.4). This pattern often develops as the leading edge of larger,

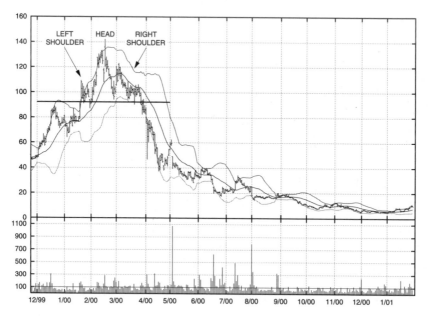

Figure 13.2 Actual head-and-shoulders top, Vishay, 250 days. Head and shoulders are rarely picture perfect; look for the key elements to clarify the picture.

longer top formations. Typically the first push will be outside the upper band, and the second push will make a new high and touch the upper band. The third push may make a marginal new high— more often not—but will fail to tag the band. Volume will diminish steadily across the pattern. This is a portrait of failing momentum, a portrait many stocks paint as their tops form. The typical building blocks would be M15s or M16s.

The first part of a head-and-shoulders formation is an M formation that consists of the left shoulder and head. M14 and M15 patterns or a blend of them would be typical. The next part is another M consisting of the head and right shoulder. M3 and M4 or M7 and M8 formations would be typical right-shoulder patterns. The final part is also an M consisting of the right shoulder and the throwback rally, typified by an M1 or M3. However, starting with the first trough after the head, you might wish to analyze the patterns as a series of Ws, as the formation now has a downside bias with a lower high and the potential for a

Figure 13.3 Head-and-shoulders top with Bollinger Bands, S1, 300 days. This is messy, but all the parts are there.

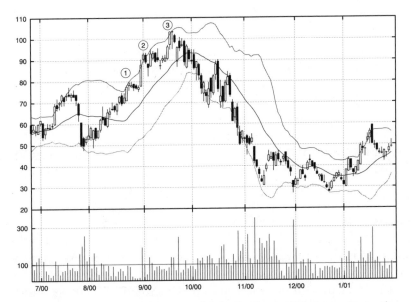

Figure 13.4 Three pushes to a high, Juniper, 200 days. Note the preponderance of black candlesticks after the final high.

lower low. A W1 or W2 would be the pattern to look for on a throwback rally.[1]

Of course, you can get even more detailed, counting each M and W as it presents itself—there would be a total of five in a head-and-shoulders pattern—and testing each for relevance. But there isn't much need to do that, except perhaps for shorter-term traders looking for setups within the context of the formation. For position traders, observing the formations as they evolve and noting their bias is generally enough.

As was the case with bottoms, often top formations such as the head-and-shoulders pattern contain smaller formations within them, especially at the next higher level of magnification. So if one is examining a head-and-shoulders pattern forming on the daily chart, look for small-scale patterns forming on the hourly charts confirming the larger pattern on the daily charts.

When you have detected a formation you think qualifies, wait for a sign of weakness to confirm your diagnosis before acting. This can be defined as a day with greater-than-average volume and greater-than-average range. There is another aspect to successful trade entry that was not discussed in the prior chapter, patience. Often after the sign of weakness there will be a countertrend rally that will provide a perfect entry point. For example, the throwback rally after the neckline is broken often provides a perfect entry point (Figure 13.5). Of course, this is true of bottoms too, but it seems clearer in relation to tops. Many professional traders require this type of setup before entering a trade, as it lets them precisely define their risk-reward relationship by setting a stop just above the top of the pullback. Very good risk-reward ratios are achievable this way.

With tops, relativity is the key, just as it was with bottoms. In many cases your outlook will need to turn cautious even though an absolute new high has been made. Really the only device for doing this successfully is Bollinger Bands. A high made outside the bands followed by a new high made inside the bands is always suspect, especially if the second (new) high fails to tag the upper band. This is the only approach we know of that can consistently warn of danger at a new high or opportunity at a new low. A particularly clear sequence is a high made outside the upper band, a pullback, a tag of the upper band, a pullback, and then a final rally that fails to achieve the upper band at all. In Part IV we'll

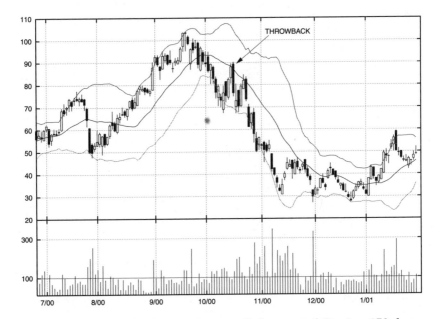

Figure 13.5   Throwback entry into a sell, Integrated Device, 150 days. Is it a right shoulder or a throwback? It doesn't matter; all that matters is the low-risk entry point it creates.

show you how to combine this information with indicators to build greater confidence in your ability to recognize important junctures for stocks.

KEY POINTS TO REMEMBER

- Tops are more complex than bottoms; hence they are harder to diagnose.
- The best known top is the head-and-shoulders.
- Three pushes to a high is a very common formation.
- The classic top shows steadily waning momentum.
- Wait for a sign of weakness.
- Look for countertrend rallies to sell.
- Potential M tops are listed each trading day on www.BollingeronBollingerBands.com.

C H A P T E R

14.

WALKING THE BANDS

We have talked about tops and bottoms, but what of sustained trends, perhaps the trickiest area when it comes to trade maintenance? The single mistake most often made with bands, envelopes, or channels is to blindly sell a tag of the upper band and/or buy a tag of the lower band. If such tags are parts of larger patterns, or are unconfirmed by indicators, they may in fact constitute buy or sell signals—but then again, they may not. *There is absolutely nothing about a tag of a band that in and of itself is a signal.*

A good example of why a tag of the upper Bollinger Band is not necessarily a sell signal comes from the U.S. stock market. In June 1998 a severe correction got under way. We pick up the action coming off the lows in October 1998 (Figure 14.1) with the correction completed and a W8 bottom in place, the S&P 500 Index entered a strong rally phase that lasted well into the next

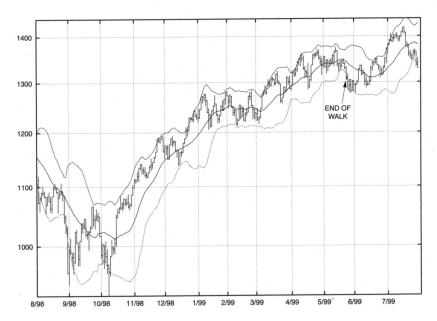

Figure 14.1 S&P 500 with Bollinger Bands, fall 1998/spring 1999. A long stroll up the upper band; the lower band is never touched.

year. This phase was characterized by any number of tags of the upper band—including one just eight days off the low. None of those tags were sell signals—at least for the intermediate-term player. Such a series of tags is called "walking the band," and it is a process that occurs frequently during sustained trends.

During an advance, walking the band is characterized by a series of tags of the upper band, usually accompanied by a number of days on which price closes outside the band (Figure 14.2). During a decline, it is the lower band that is frequently tagged or undercut. *These closes outside the bands are continuation signals, not reversal signals.* They may become the first part of a pattern that leads to a reversal signal, but usually they are not in and of themselves reversals. Typically a pattern will develop with an unconfirmed peak or trough occurring inside the bands generating a signal, but such a pattern may not occur until after many continuation signals have been generated.

The open forms[1] of many volume indicators—especially Intraday Intensity (II) or Accumulation Distribution (AD)—are

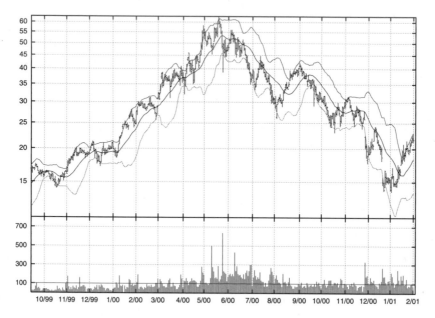

Figure 14.2 Walk up the band followed by an M top, Vishay, 350 days. Closes outside of the bands are continuation signals.

very useful in helping to diagnose periods in which price walks the band (Figure 14.3). This is because these indicators tend to act like trend descriptors in their open forms and can be compared directly with price more easily than oscillators when the market is trending. To enhance this comparison, plot II or AD in the same clip as price, but with a separate scale.

The closed forms of II or AD are very useful in that tags of the bands should be accompanied by similar action in the indicator (Figure 14.4). A tag accompanied by an opposing reading from 21-day II% is an action signal associated with the end of a trend. Be especially careful about small divergences. It can be enough for the indicators to get into the neighborhood of their prior highs. For example, if 21-day II% is consistently getting into the low 20 percent range on each leg up, a leg that only carries it to 19 or 20 percent may be a warning, but it is not likely a sell signal—at least not yet. The first divergences are usually just warnings that will be followed by clearer, more meaningful divergences later if a top or bottom is forming.

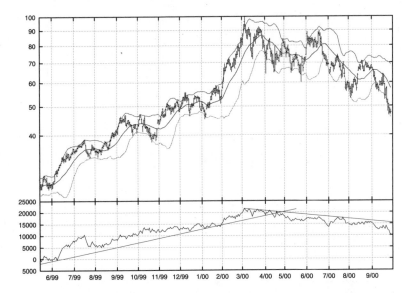

Figure 14.3 Walk up the band with Intraday Intensity, open, Texas Instruments, 350 days. Note the indicator turns down confirming price action.

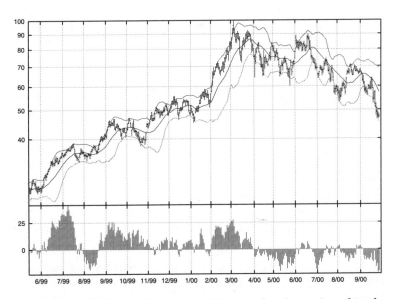

Figure 14.4 Walk up the band with Intraday Intensity, closed, Texas Instruments, 350 days. Indicator positive until top forms, then negative thereafter.

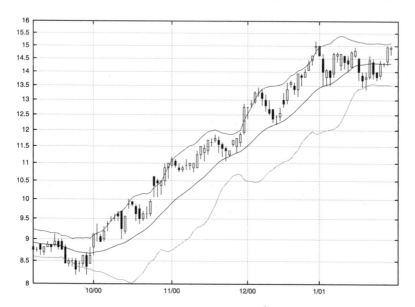

Figure 14.5   The average as support, Archer Daniels, 100 days. Support from a well-chosen average defines the trend.

If the average selected is well suited to the stock, that is, if it is descriptive of the intermediate trend, then it will tend to provide support on pullbacks during a walk up or down the bands (Figure 14.5). These can be excellent entry, add-on, or reentry points. As was the case with tops, these points offer superior risk-reward relationships, as you will know quite quickly if you are wrong—and the potential if you are right is great.

Often a walk up or down a band will consist of three primary legs. Many different disciplines, including R. N. Elliott's wave theory, have suggested that three legs up or down interrupted by corrections is the typical pattern within a trend (Figure 14.6); in a reaction expect two legs interrupted by one countermove.[2] While these are indeed useful guidelines that can help diagnose a walk along the bands or other phases of market activity, they cannot be relied upon in an absolute manner, as the number of legs in a trend will frequently be a number other—often larger—than three. When that is the case, a weakening of the ability for price to get outside the bands will often warn that the advance or decline is in its waning days.

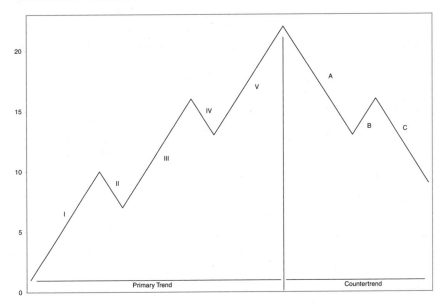

Figure 14.6   Basic Elliott wave pattern.

If Elliott rules or guidelines are employed, it is very important not to get adamant about them. Always go with what actually transpires in the marketplace, not with what you expect to transpire. Disciplines that rely on rigid rules, or exact depictions of the structural aspects of trading, will lead their adherents astray just often enough to do serious damage to their capital.

Though not the subject of this book, approaches such as R. N. Elliott's or W. D. Gann's do contain elements of truth; however, they are not the totalities they are sold as to the masses. By all means use their rules—they are based on long observation of the markets and contain a great deal of wisdom—but use them carefully. The markets don't know they are supposed to follow the rules and often break them out of ignorance, leaving dogmatic adherents without guidance in the best case, or with the wrong guidance in the worst case.

There are no simple answers to the problems of investing. Investing is a tough and complex job; it has always been and will always be so. Simple systems will not suffice. For every wave count there is an alternate clamoring for attention. For every date, there is another, more important, date. Setups where the risk and reward parameters can be quantified are the only reasonable way to go. The use of ancillary data and/or methods to improve confidence is fine. Just be careful about what you use and how you use it.

Every idea presented in this book can be quantified, and we urge you to do so, just as we urge you to quantify all your other tools. Indeed, such a quantification process is the first step toward building up enough confidence to execute successfully. Why hasn't this been done for you? Because it can't be. Only you know your risk-reward criteria. Only you know whether an approach will work for you. The world of system testing assumes that you will be able to execute the system, but the fact is you are going to second-guess any system—right from the very start. One system may be too volatile, another too slow. The path to success is to survey the ideas presented in this book, choose those that are intuitively correct to you, and then test them on the stocks you trade, in the way you trade, and see if they work for you. It is one thing for someone to baldly assert that something works and quite another for it to work for you.

If you want a simple approach, take one of the three methods presented here and give it a try. Modify it to suit your needs and proceed. However, a better chance for success lies in integrating the ideas presented in this book into your already existing approach. That way you benefit from what you already know and what this book has to offer.

(In addition to the prescreened lists on www.BollingeronBollingerBands.com, the professional section of www.EquityTrader.com presents daily lists of stocks that are walking up or down the Bollinger Bands.)

KEY POINTS TO REMEMBER

- Walks up and down the bands are quite common.
- There is nothing about a tag of a band that is a buy or sell in and of itself.
- Indicators can help distinguish between a confirmed tag and an unconfirmed one.
- The average may provide support and entry points during a sustained trend.

CHAPTER

15

THE SQUEEZE

So far we have examined the process of diagnosing tops and bottoms with Bollinger Bands and looked into the dynamics of walking the bands. In Part IV we'll add indicators to the decision matrix, but first there is one more important use of the bands in the stand-alone mode, The Squeeze.

The Squeeze draws more questions than any other aspect of Bollinger Bands and is without doubt the most popular Bollinger Bands topic. There is something about a dramatic and/or prolonged contraction of the bands and the subsequent explosion of activity that captures the attention. First, we'll delve into what The Squeeze is and present a tool to measure it. Then we'll present some background material on volatility and look at some ideas on how to trade The Squeeze.

Bollinger Bands are driven by volatility, and The Squeeze is a pure reflection of that volatility. When volatility falls to

Table 15-1. BandWidth Formula

(Upper BB − lower BB)/middle BB

historically low levels, The Squeeze is on. An indicator called BandWidth (see Table 15.1) was created in order to measure The Squeeze.[1] BandWidth depicts volatility as a function of the average (Figure 15.1). As such it is comparable from security to security, across time, and across markets. As we have seen earlier, volatility is highly variable over time. It is precisely this variability that is the key to The Squeeze.

The Squeeze has several definitions. The simplest one—one that will do admirably for our purposes—is that a Squeeze is triggered when BandWidth drops to its lowest level in six months.[2]

For some years there has been an academic theory in circulation that suggests that while price is neither cyclical nor forecastable, volatility is both. (You might want to reread Chapter 9,

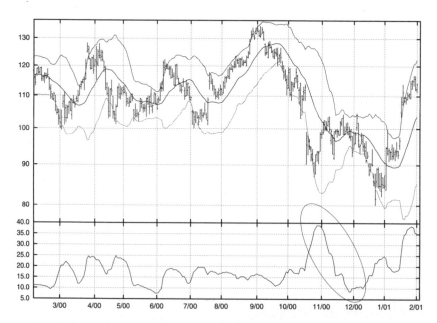

Figure 15.1 Bollinger Bands and BandWidth, IBM, 250 days. BandWidth falls from over 40 percent to less than 10 percent in 20 days.

"Statistics," now.) The bit about volatility is right on, though price does exhibit elements of cyclicity and forecastability.

For example, in the U.S. stock market there are strong seasonal trends. Both an annual and a four-year pattern are quite clear and can be used to great advantage. Indeed, the four-year cycle can be used to explain much of the variability in the annual cycle. From quite a different vantage point, John Ehlers has shown that commodity prices contain useful cyclical information in the short term.

So, while the part of the proposition that suggests price is neither cyclical nor forecastable seems overstated, there is substantial evidence that volatility both exhibits cycles and is forecastable that confirms the second half of the theory. For example, examine Figure 15.2, which shows Treasury bond futures and their BandWidth. It demonstrates clearly a 19-day volatility cycle, a cycle that often marks important junctures. It also demonstrates quite clearly the most important aspect of this theory of volatility, that low volatility begets high volatility, and high volatility begets low. If it is a quiet day, expect a storm. If it is a stormy day, expect quiet.

Time and again, we see The Squeeze in action. A consolidation begins. The resulting trading range narrows dramatically. The average flattens and now tracks right down the center of the data structure. The Bollinger Bands begin to tighten around the price structure (Figure 15.3). The stage is set. Now we turn to our indicators. Is volume picking up on up days? Is Accumulation Distribution turning up? Does the range narrow on down days? What is the relationship of the open to the close? Each piece of evidence helps forecast the direction of the resolution. Watch carefully for news, as news is often the catalyst.

Traders beware! There is a trick to The Squeeze, an odd turning of the wheel that you need to be aware of, the head fake (Figure 15.4). Often as the end of a Squeeze nears, price will stage a short fake-out move, and then abruptly turn and surge in the direction of the emerging trend. The head fake was first noted in the S&P 500 Index futures many years ago, and numerous examples have been seen since.

To deal with the head fake, you can wait for the move to develop sufficiently so that there is little question about the nature of the emerging trend. Or if you want to trade The Squeeze right

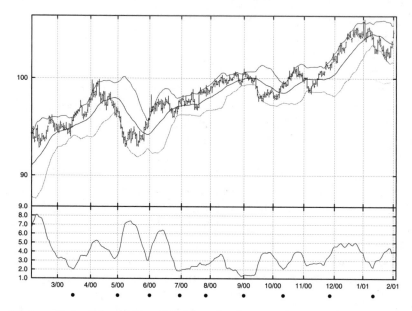

Figure 15.2 T-bond BandWidth, 250 days. The volatility cycle is really clear in the bond market.

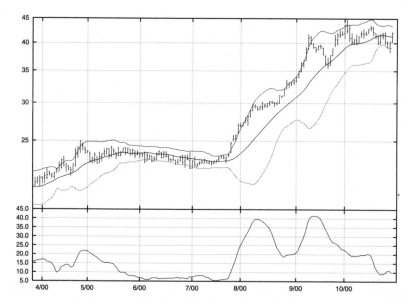

Figure 15.3 The Squeeze and a breakout, PPL, 150 days. Low volatility begets high volatility.

Figure 15.4 The Squeeze, a head fake, and a breakout, Adobe, 100 days. First one way then the other.

from the beginning, you can take an initial position in the direction of the fake. Then use a technique that sets stop-loss orders behind the position, such as Welles Wilder's Parabolic, to reverse to the opposite direction if it is indeed a fake-out.[3] This is called using a trailing stop. It is a technique favored by commodity traders whose systems are often in the market full time, reversing from long to short as price moves evolve.

If The Squeeze is a reflection of low volatility and low volatility invites high volatility to the table, then there should be an opposite function, a reverse Squeeze, The Expansion, and there is. However, just as bottoms are clearer than tops, a Squeeze is clearer than an Expansion.

An Expansion generates an important rule: When a powerful trend is born, volatility expands so much that the lower band will turn down in an uptrend or the upper band will turn up in a downtrend. When that happens, it is an Expansion, and when the Expansion reverses, the odds are very high that the trend is at an end (Figure 15.5). That doesn't necessarily mean the entire move is over. Another leg could easily materialize. But it does mean that

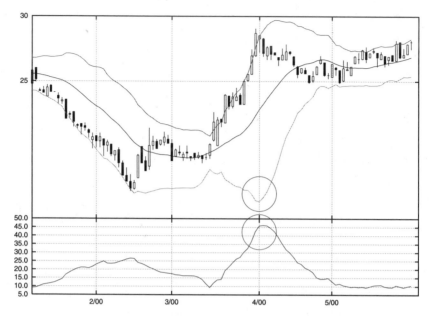

Figure 15.5 The reversal of an expansion, the end of a trend, American Financial Group, 100 days. Maximum volatility at peak price intensity.

the current leg is most likely over. The realistic expectation is now for a consolidation or a reversal, not the continuation of the trend everybody is hoping for. From a strategic point of view, this is the time to sell options against existing positions, as option premiums will be very high.

In the next chapter, we'll explore a way to exploit The Squeeze in the first of our methods, a volatility breakout system.

KEY POINTS TO REMEMBER

- Low volatility begets high volatility.
- High volatility begets low volatility.
- Beware the head fake.
- Use indicators to forecast direction.
- Squeeze lists are available on www.BollingeronBollinger-Bands.com.

16

METHOD I: VOLATILITY BREAKOUT

The three methods of using Bollinger Bands presented in this book illustrate three completely different philosophical approaches. Which one is for you we cannot say, as it is really a matter of what you are comfortable with. Try each out. Customize them to suit your tastes. Look at the trades they generate and see if you can live with them.

Though these techniques were developed on daily charts—the primary time frame we operate in—short-term traders may deploy them on five-minute bar charts, swing traders may focus on hourly or daily charts, while investors may use them on weekly charts. There is really no material difference as long as each is tuned to fit the user's criteria for risk and reward, and each is tested on the universe of securities the user trades, in the way the user trades.

Why the repeated emphasis on customization and fitting of risk and reward parameters? Because no system, no matter how good it is, will be used if the user isn't comfortable with it. If you do not suit yourself, you will find out quickly that these approaches will not suit you.

"If these methods work so well, why do you teach them?" This is a frequent question, and the answer is always the same. First, I teach because I love to teach. Second, and perhaps most important, because I learn as I teach. In researching and preparing the material for this book, I learned quite a bit, and I learned even more in the process of writing it.

"Will these methods still work after they are published?" The question of continued effectiveness seems troublesome to many, but it is not really. These techniques will remain useful until the market structure changes sufficiently to render them moot. The reason that effectiveness is not destroyed—no matter how widely an approach is taught—is that we are all individuals. If an identical trading system was taught to 100 people, a month later not more than two or three, if that many, would be using it as it was taught. The people would have taken it and modified it to suit their individual tastes, and incorporated it into their unique way of doing things. In short, no matter how specific or declarative a book gets, every reader will walk away from reading it with unique ideas and approaches, and that, as they say, is a good thing.

The greatest myth about Bollinger Bands is that you are supposed to sell at the upper band and buy at the lower band. It can work that way, but it doesn't have to. In Method I we'll actually buy when the upper band is exceeded and short when the lower band is broken to the downside.[1] In Method II we'll buy on strength as we approach the upper band only if an indicator confirms and sell on weakness as the lower band is approached, again only if confirmed by our indicator. In Method III we'll buy near the lower band, using a W pattern and an indicator to clarify the setup or we'll sell near the upper band on a series of tags accompanied by a weakening indicator. Then a variation that relies on nonconfirmed band tags to identify buys and sells will be presented.

Method I, also known as The Squeeze, anticipates high volatility by taking advantage of the cyclical nature of volatility and looking for extremely low volatility as a precursor of high volatility.

Now, for Method I. Years ago the late Bruce Babcock of *Commodity Traders Consumers Review* interviewed me for that publication. After the interview, we chatted for a while, and the interviewing gradually reversed; and it came out that his favorite commodity trading approach was the volatility breakout. I could hardly believe my ears. Here is the fellow who had examined more trading systems—and done so rigorously—than anyone else, with the possible exception of John Hill of Futures Truth, and he was saying that his approach of choice to trading was the volatility-breakout system? The very approach that I thought best for trading after a lot of investigation?

Perhaps the most elegant direct application of Bollinger Bands is a volatility-breakout system. These systems have been around a long time and exist in many varieties and forms. The earliest breakout systems used simple averages of the highs and lows, often shifted up or down a bit. As time went on, average true range was frequently a factor.[2]

There is no real way of knowing when volatility, as we use it now, was incorporated as a factor, but one would surmise that one day someone noticed that breakout signals worked better when the averages, bands, envelopes, etc., were closer together, and so the volatility-breakout system was born. (Certainly the risk-reward parameters are better aligned when the bands are narrow, a major factor in any system.)

Our version of the venerable volatility-breakout system utilizes BandWidth to set the precondition and then takes a position when a breakout occurs. There are two choices for a stop or exit for this approach. First, Welles Wilder's Parabolic,[3] a simple but elegant concept. In the case of a stop for a buy signal, the initial stop is set just below the range of the breakout formation and then incremented upward each day the trade is open. Just the opposite is true for a sell. For those willing to pursue larger profits than those afforded by the relatively conservative Parabolic approach, a tag of the opposite band is an excellent exit signal. This allows for corrections along the way and results in longer trades. So, in a buy use a tag of the lower band as an exit, and in a sell use a tag of the upper band as an exit.

The major problem with successfully implementing Method I is a head fake (Figure 16.1)—discussed in the prior chapter. The term came from hockey, but it is familiar in many other arenas

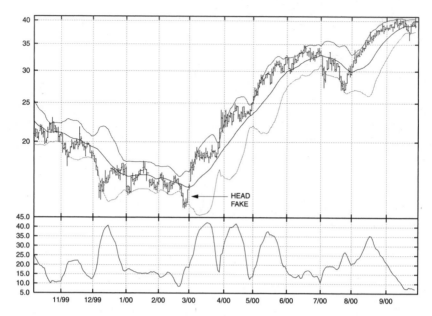

Figure 16.1 Head fake, EOG Resources, 250 days. The head fake spells opportunity for the canny trader.

as well. The idea is a player with the puck skates up the ice toward an opponent. As he skates, he turns his head in preparation to pass the defender; as soon as the defenseman commits, he turns his body the other way and safely snaps his shot. Coming out of a Squeeze, stocks often do the same; they'll first feint in the wrong direction and then make the real move. Typically what you'll see is a Squeeze, followed by a band tag, followed in turn by the real move. Most often this will occur within the bands and you won't get a breakout signal until after the real move is under way. However, if you have tightened the parameters for the bands as so many who use this approach do, you may find yourself with the occasional small whipsaw before the real trade appears.

Some stocks, indices, etc., are more prone to head fakes than others. Take a look at past Squeezes for the item you are considering and see if they involved head fakes. Once a faker…

For those who are willing to take a nonmechanical approach trading head fakes, the easiest strategy is to wait until a Squeeze occurs—the precondition is set—and then look for the first move away from the trading range. Trade half a position the first strong day in the opposite direction of the head fake adding to the position when the breakout occurs and using a parabolic or opposite band tag stop to keep from being hurt.

Where head fakes aren't a problem, or the band parameters aren't set tight enough for those that do occur to be a problem, you can trade Method I straight up. Just wait for a Squeeze and go with the first breakout.

Volume indicators can really add value. In the phase before the head fake, look for a volume indicator such as Intraday Intensity or Accumulation Distribution to give a hint regarding the ultimate resolution. Money Flow Index is another indicator that can be used to improve success and confidence. These are all volume indicators and are taken up in Part IV.

The parameters for a volatility breakout system based on The Squeeze can be the standard parameters: 20-day average and ±2 standard deviation bands. This is true because in this phase of activity the bands are quite close together and thus the triggers are very close by. However, some short-term traders may want to shorten the average a bit, say to 15 periods, and tighten the bands a bit, say to 1.5 standard deviations.

There is one other parameter that can be set, the look-back period for the Squeeze. The longer you set the look-back period—recall that the default is six months—the greater the compression you'll achieve and the more explosive the setups will be. However, there will be fewer of them. There is always a price to pay it seems.

Method I first detects compression through The Squeeze and then looks for range expansion to occur and goes with it. An awareness of head fakes and volume indicator confirmation can add significantly to the record of this approach. Screening a reasonable-size universe of stocks—at least several hundred—ought to find at least several candidates to evaluate on any given day.

Look for your Method I setups carefully and then follow them as they evolve. There is something about looking at a large number of these setups, especially with volume indicators, that instructs the eye and thus informs the future selection process as no hard-and-fast rules ever can. Figures 16.2 to 16.6 give you an idea of what to look for.

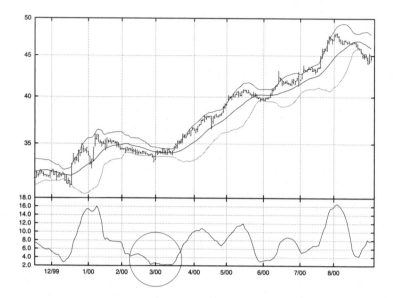

Figure 16.2 Method I example, AvalonBay Communities, 200 days. A 2 percent BandWidth—a real Squeeze.

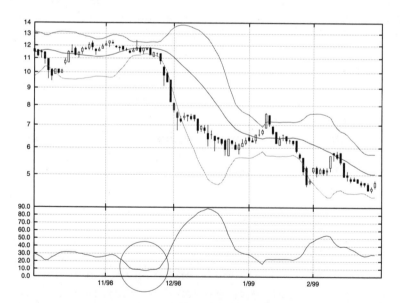

Figure 16.3 Method I example, Ocean Energy, 100 days. A 10 percent BandWidth is still a Squeeze. Look for the lowest reading in six months, not an absolute level.

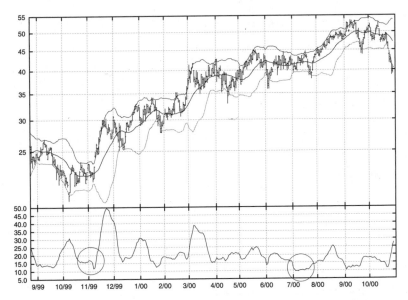

Figure 16.4 Method I example, Noble Drilling, 300 days. A Squeeze can be high or low on the chart, it doesn't matter.

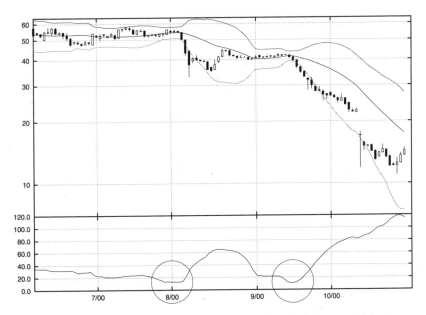

Figure 16.5 Method I example, Pinnacle Holdings, 100 days. Squeeze, and Squeeze again.

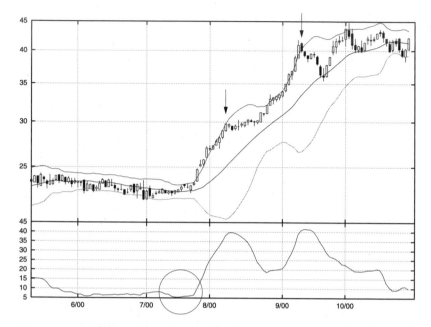

Figure 16.6 Method I example, PPL Corp., 120 days. The first leg is 5 to 40 percent, then over 40 percent on the second leg. Note the peaks mark important highs.

KEY POINTS TO REMEMBER

- Use the Squeeze as a setup.
- Then go with an expansion in volatility.
- Beware the head fake.
- Use volume indicators for direction clues.
- Adjust the parameters to suit yourself.
- Lists of Method I candidates are available on www.Bollinger-onBollingerBands.com.

PART
IV

BOLLINGER BANDS
WITH INDICATORS

Part IV adds indicators to the analytical mix with the focus on volume indicators. The focus in this part is creating a rigorous methodology where the risk-reward equation is in our favor. Part IV concludes with the final two trading methods—one that picks reversals and a trend-following method.

133

C H A P T E R

17

BOLLINGER BANDS
AND INDICATORS

The real power of Bollinger Bands becomes evident when they are combined with indicators. The indicators of choice are volume indicators, and the preferred operating mode is comparing price action within the bands to indicator action (Figure 17.1).

Price-indicator comparisons can result in either a confirmation or a nonconfirmation. An example of a confirmation is a tag of the upper band combined with a sufficiently strong indicator (Figure 17.2). If you have a long position and price tags the upper band—a situation in which many would consider selling—consult your indicator. If the indicator is sufficiently strong, take the tag to be a confirmation of your position. (If the indicator is weaker than at a prior tag, consider this an early warning signal.)

An example of a nonconfirmation is a tag of the lower band accompanied by a positive indicator reading, which constitutes a classic buy signal (Figure 17.3). For example, if you were looking

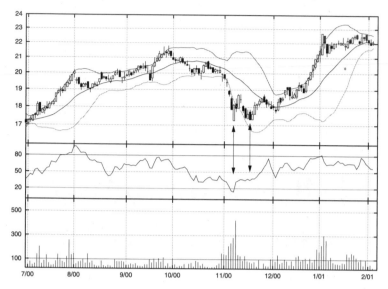

Figure 17.1 BB, MFI, and normalized volume, Healthcare Realty, 150 days. Price retests its prior low, but MFI is dramatically higher—a classic positive signal.

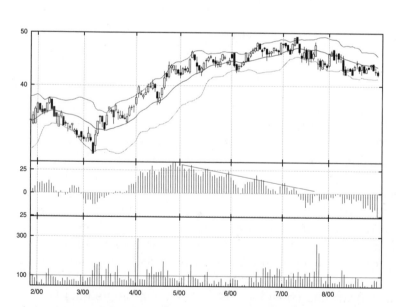

Figure 17.2 BB, AD%, and normalized volume, Pfizer, 120 days. Note the change in character of the oscillator as we transition from an advance to a decline.

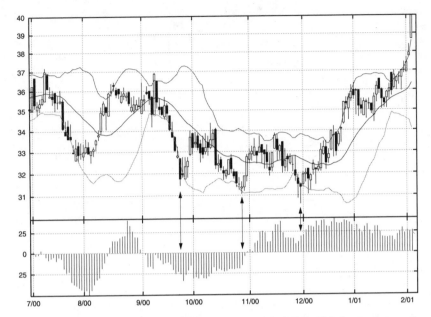

Figure 17.3 BB, Intraday Intensity %, Ashland Oil, 150 days. A tag of the lower band, a new low in price, and positive II% equal a great opportunity.

for a stock to purchase, and among the stocks you monitored you found one that tagged the lower band accompanied by a positive volume oscillator reading, you'd have a reversal purchase candidate. If this were the second tag and therefore a potential W bottom, you would have supporting evidence for the successful completion of a reversal to a positive trend. Now all you would need is a sign of strength to confirm the reversal.

An example that is neither fish nor fowl is a band tag accompanied by a neutral indicator reading (Figure 17.4). If you are long and price tags the upper band with the indicator neutral, take that as a warning to tighten up your stops or exercise increased vigilance. If the indicator is negative, it is an outright sell signal.

A very good example of confirmations is a walk up the upper Bollinger Band accompanied by strong indicator readings (Figure 17.5). The typical sequence is that during the sustained portion of the trend, each tag of the upper band is accompanied by a strong indicator reading. As the top is approached, band

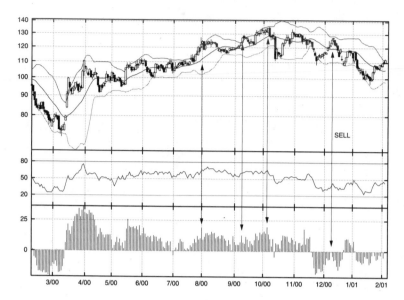

Figure 17.4 BB, MFI, and AD%, Marsh & McLennan, 150 days. Several tags of the upper band accompanied by weak indicator readings suggest caution, but a sell doesn't come until late on the chart.

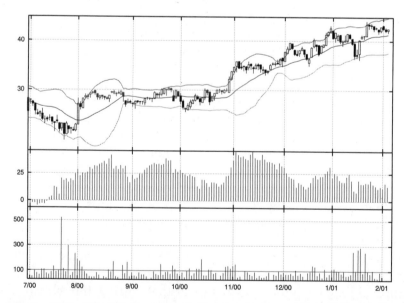

Figure 17.5 BB, II%, and normalized volume, walk up the band, Sabre Holdings, 150 days. Tag after tag confirmed.

tags are accompanied by a succession of weaker indicator readings, resulting in a series of cautions, until you finally get an outright sell.

Strong stocks are often hard to hold onto. Staying with strong stocks during a series of upper Bollinger Band tags can be a nerve-wracking process. But in the presence of indicator confirmation, strong stocks should be given the benefit of the doubt.

Earlier we looked at M and W patterns and how Bollinger Bands could be used to clarify them. This relative framework allowed you to act even if a new low or high occurred in the second half of the pattern. The key was *relative* highs and lows, that is, highs and lows as a function of the Bollinger Bands, not of absolute price levels. Here we consider a second qualifier, an indicator that acts to increase our confidence.

Take a W2 bottom as an example. The second leg down makes a new low, but if that new low does not break the lower band as did the first low, you now have a relative W4 and should be ready to buy on the first strong up day (Figure 17.6). *Buying shortly after a*

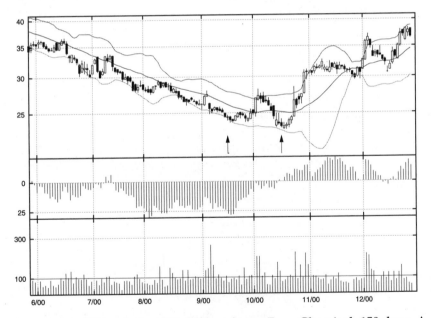

Figure 17.6 W2, relative W4, II% confirms, Dow Chemical, 150 days. A new absolute low in price but no new relative low; plus the indicator turns positive.

new low is made can be very scary, but the fear can be reduced and confidence increased if the indicator used for confirmation does not go to a new low. In that situation we have two positive signals: one, no new low relative to the bands and, two, indicator confirmation. A sign of strength such as an up day on above-average volume and above-average range would be the third confirmation.

The natural thing to ask is, If two pieces of confirmation are better than one, why not use three or even four? No reason at all why you can't. In fact, using more than one indicator for confirmation can improve your results. However, a problem arises if the indicators are collinear, which is to say, if the indicators are all singing the same song. That is the great trap of multicollinearity—several series containing very similar information used as though they were separate, independent inputs. Many a sorry trader has been caught in this trap, some completely unaware.

The multicollinearity trap can be easily avoided; all that is required is a bit of discipline. Use only one indicator from each category, one momentum indicator, one trend indicator, one volume indicator, etc. (see Table 17.1)—similar to the approach of certain American Chinese restaurant menus, one from column a, one from column b. . . with no substitutions allowed. Using three different momentum indicators drops you directly into the collinearity trap; they are all saying the same thing derived from the same source. If the waiter were doing his job, he wouldn't take this order, but most market software is not that smart.

It is possible to use indicators from the same category and avoid the multicollinearity trap if those indicators are not closely correlated with each other. But this requires testing and careful consideration, and should be avoided unless there is an overriding

Table 17.1 Indicator Categories with Two Examples of Each

Category	Example Indicators
Momentum	Rate of change, stochastics
Trend	Linear regression, MACD
Sentiment	Survey, put-call ratio
Volume (open)	Intraday Intensity, Accumulation Distribution
Volume (closed)	Money Flow Index, Volume-Weighted MACD
Overbought/oversold	Commodity Channel Index, RSI

reason to do so; e.g., indicators from other categories are not available (substitutions allowed, but at a price).

Volume and sentiment indicators fit particularly well into a diversification strategy to avoid the multicollinearity trap. Why? Because they introduce new, independent variables that are probably not already considered in the analysis and are therefore unlikely to be collinear with other elements of the analysis. Momentum and trend indicators, being directly derived from price, are already duplicating some of the data the eye gleans from the charts and are therefore less useful than volume or sentiment indicators.

Another very dangerous indicator trap is sycophantism. Dictionary.com defines sycophant as "A servile self-seeker who attempts to win favor by flattering influential people."[1] The last thing you want is indicators that behave like sycophants, flattering you by confirming your opinion, telling you what you already know, or worse, what you wish to hear. The time that this trap most often bites is when the user looks through a number of indicators until one is found that confirms the analysis. Desperate for a reason to make a trade, confirmatory evidence is eagerly sought after—never a good idea to start with—and the sycophant trap strikes. To avoid the sycophant trap, choose your approach or tools before the trade and then stick with them. Other indicators appropriate to the situation can be consulted, but avoid hunting expeditions for confirmatory evidence.

It is very important that you choose your indicators and do whatever testing you are going to do *before* you start looking for trades. Having selected the analytical tools, create a template(s) to use for your analysis. Figure 17.7 is a good example of a basic template. The top clip is a log-scaled candlestick chart with Bollinger Bands and a 50-day average. Log scaling makes percentage changes comparable anywhere on the chart, candlesticks highlight the important relationship of the open to the close, Bollinger Bands provide a relative definition of high and low, and the 50-day average gives a sense of trend. Overlaid in the same clip but plotted with a separate scale is relative strength—the ratio of the stock to the S&P 500, which gives a feel for how the stock is doing in relation to the market. In the chart clip directly below the price clip is 21-day Accumulation Distribution plotted as an oscillator; this is our indicator for confirming price action. Finally, in the

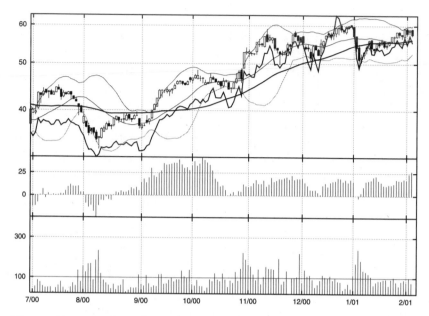

Figure 17.7 Analytical Template I, CVS, 150 days. Use tags setup regularly. Adding the relative strength to the market really helps.

bottom clip, volume is plotted as a function of its 50-day average, which is useful for clarifying price patterns.

Another example of a useful template starts with a log-scaled candlestick chart and then plots Accumulation Distribution as a line in the same clip as price, but on its own scale (Figure 17.8). Then moving average convergence/divergence (MACD) is plotted in a separate clip. A clip with normalized volume completes this stack.

Having built a template(s) that suits your analytical approach, now review your stocks looking for setups. Then make your decisions without introducing extraneous, untested factors. Failure to follow these guidelines, or another rigorous methodology, can lead you along the path to destruction via emotions. *Pick your indicators and create your analysis templates before you trade!*

A related matter to the idea of picking indicators, building templates, and sticking with them is that your indicator choices must derive from first principles; i.e., you must know why they work[2] and what test results you are expecting before you

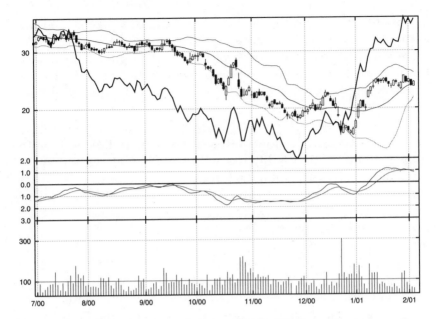

Figure 17.8 Analytical Template II, AT&T, 150 days. A stronger focus on volume indicators in the setup really helps pick the low here.

test and choose. Using indicators not grounded firmly in practical considerations and not fully understood will result in insufficient confidence to execute the system when the times get rough, or, for that matter, when the times get too good! It is at the extremes that our emotions impact our actions to the greatest degree. Unless you have the highest level of confidence in your approach, you'll find it impossible to stick to it when the emotional climate becomes volatile.

All the tools and techniques presented in this book arise from first principles. That is, they are firmly footed in the underlying reality of the marketplace and their motive forces are well understood. An example of developing a technique from first principles starts with the idea that volume precedes price. One could build an indicator based on that idea by comparing volume with its 50-day average during a period in which price was building a base, theorizing that there ought to be a coincident bias to firming prices and firming volume before the base is completed and the breakout occurs. Having laid out the theoretical grounds, formulate the indicator and test it to see whether you are correct.

If you are correct and the indicator behaves as expected, you may employ the idea. Purist advocates of first principles will argue that there shouldn't be any modification to the original formulation, but in my opinion there is no need to be so hidebound. Test and adjust and optimize carefully, taking care to avoid the usual traps, and you should be fine.

Optimization is a topic well beyond the scope of this book, but one can't discuss indicators and systems without touching on the subject. Optimization is littered with pitfalls that can entrap the wary investor. While optimization can be a useful tool, it is often abused, sometimes unknowingly. The product of this abuse is merely a good description of the data rather than a useful tool. The abuse of optimization is another way into the sycophant trap that was discussed above.

Optimization is the process of finding the "best" parameter(s) for a given approach. These days, optimization is usually done by computer, but it was done by hand before PCs were common. The simplest and most common optimization is the moving-average crossover. The optimization program starts with some small value for the moving-average length and then calculates all the buys and sells based on crossings of the average, and reports the profitability, number of trades, worst loss, best gain, etc. The process is then repeated for a slightly longer average, and again for a slightly longer average, and so on, until some terminal value is reached. The results of all the runs are tabulated, with various statistics computed that allow the user to see what the most profitable parameter(s) was.

The optimization process can quickly get quite complex. For example, let's examine optimizing a system using Bollinger Bands and one indicator. Let's say you vary the average length by 2s from 10 to 50 (21 trials) and the indicator period by 2s from 4 to 20 (9 trials)—21 times 9 equals 189 tests. Now vary the width of the bands and the threshold for the indicator, say by just two levels (3 trials for each) and you have 1701 trials—189 times 3 times 3. You can see how it is possible to get mired quickly.

Sectioning is one way to avoid the most common optimization pitfall—simply building a good description of the data on hand. Break your histories into several different sections and perform your testing independently on each. For example, if you had 10 years of data from 1990 through 1999, you might optimize in three sections of three years each, using the first year of each section as a run-up period for the indicators and the last two years for optimization, 1990 through 1992, 1992 through 1994, and 1994 through 1996. Then test the results for consistency on the most recent period, 1996 through 1999, again allowing the first year for run-up and testing on the final three years that hadn't been seen in the prior optimization runs. The results from each section should be quite similar; the greater the similarity, the higher the confidence you can have. This is called *robustness*.

Another tack is to break the items you are testing into several different groups, perhaps with different characteristics, e.g., volatile versus stable, growth versus value, small versus large, or low price versus high price. Look for consistency in results. The idea is to assure that you actually have a window onto important analytical information, not just a good description of what worked then, or what works for those stocks. One last test is to see whether the parameters you have chosen are robust: Change your parameters by small, but meaningful, amounts and retest. If you have a robust method, the results of the tests should again be consistent; i.e., if you find 20 periods to be optimal, then 18 and 22 periods should produce similar results.

Next we'll look at volume indicators, and then we'll consider two methods based on indicators confirming price action in and around the Bollinger Bands.

KEY POINTS TO REMEMBER

- Use indicators to confirm band tags.
- Volume indicators are preferred.
- Avoid collinearity.
- Choose your indicators before the trade.
- Use prebuilt templates for analysis.
- If you must optimize, do so carefully.

18

VOLUME
INDICATORS

For those of you who want to fine-tune or alter either our methods or your own methods, this section provides the background information you'll need to do so effectively. Those of you suffering from math fright may skip the second half of this chapter, but do read at least the next few paragraphs.

Volume indicators are the most important group of indicators for the technician. They get right at the heart of the supply-demand equation while introducing an independent variable, volume, into the analytical mix. Underlying all volume indicators to some extent is the concept that volume precedes price. For example, during a base, smart investors are accumulating stock in anticipation of a rally; or in the latter stages of a rally, smart money starts to get out before the top is in.

Volume indicators suffer from terrible nomenclature problems; they are rarely referred to by the same name in any two programs.

So to avoid confusion the indicators and authors are set out in Table 18.1. The formulas and construction of the recommended indicators are set out in Table 18.3 on page 148. This way you can compare these formulations with those of the analytical software you are using to determine which indicator names to use.

In order to understand how best to implement indicators of any kind, thorough knowledge of the indicators themselves is needed. This can only be accomplished by gaining real understanding not only of the calculation methods, but of the motive forces behind the indicators as well. As shown in Table 18.2, there are four basic categories of volume indicators based on the computational methods used to calculate the indicators. We'll start with a brief survey roughly in order of their creation and then give the details for the four most important indicators. We'll conclude with some general comments on deploying these powerful tools.

The first category of volume indicators includes On Balance Volume (OBV) and Volume-Price Trend (V-PT) and is characterized by calculations driven by period-over-period price change.

Table 18.1   Volume Indicators and Their Authors

Indicator	Author
On Balance Volume	Frank Vignola, Joe Granville
Volume-Price Trend	David Markstein
Negative and Positive Volume Indices	Paul and Richard Dysart
Intraday Intensity	David Bostian
Accumulation Distribution	Larry Williams
Money Flow Index	Gene Quong and Avram Soudek
Volume-Weighted MACD	Buff Dormeier

Table 18.2   Categories of Volume Indicators

Category	Examples
Periodic price change	On Balance Volume, Volume-Price Trend
Periodic volume change	Negative and Positive Volume Indices
Intraperiod structure	Intraday Intensity, Accumulation Distribution
Volume weighting	Money Flow Index, Volume-Weighted MACD

OBV looks at whether the close is up or down, while V-PT considers the percentage change. The second category, which includes the Positive Volume Indices (PVI) and Negative Volume Indices (NVI), is the logical opposite of the first category. Here the change in volume is used to parse price to form the indicator rather than the change in price being used to parse volume. For example, NVI changes only in periods when volume drops from the prior period. The third category relies on an examination of each period's internal data to drive the indicators and includes Intraday Intensity, based on where we close in the range, and Accumulation Distribution, based on the relationship of the high and low to the range. These indicators have no reference to prior periods. The fourth category uses volume to inform existing indicators. Included are the Money Flow Index, a version of Welles Wilder's Relative Strength Index, and Volume-Weighted (VW) MACD, a version of Gerald Appel's MACD. Here, the volume during the calculation period modifies traditional price-based indicators, creating powerful volume-weighted hybrids (see Table 18.3).

It is the third and fourth categories, intraperiod structure and volume weighting, that are most interesting and useful in today's trading environment, and it is those that we will explore here, though perhaps the Positive Volume Index deserves some attention too. Let's start with Intraday Intensity.

Intraday Intensity (Figure 18.1) looks at traders as they tip their hands toward the end of the day via a formula that evaluates

Table 18.3 Volume Indicator Formulas

On Balance Volume = volume ∗ the sign of the change
Volume-Price Trend = volume ∗ percentage change
Negative Volume Index = if volume falls, accumulate price change
Positive Volume Index = if volume rises, accumulate price change
Intraday Intensity = (2 ∗ close − high − low)/(high − low) ∗ volume
Accumulation Distribution = (close − open)/(high − low) ∗ volume
MFI = 100 − 100/(1 + positive price ∗ volume sum/negative
                price ∗ volume sum)
VWMACD = 12-period volume-weighted average of the last
                − 26-period volume-weighted average of the last
VWMACD signal line = 9-period exponential average VWMACD

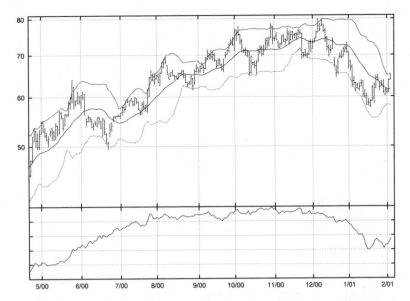

Figure 18.1 Intraday Intensity, Hartford Insurance, 200 days. This is what a great indicator ought to do. Confirmation all along, then a new high in price but not for the indicator.

to 1 if we close at the top of the range, 0 if we close in the midst of the range, and −1 when we close at the bottom of the range. The idea is that as the day progresses, traders are increasingly anxious to complete their orders and push prices in the direction of their order book. So a trader with a large sell order, say from a portfolio manager, that he is unable to complete in the course of the day will pound prices lower as the close nears, looking to fill his quota and closing the stock near the lows of the day, driving the indicator lower as he does so.

Accumulation Distribution (Figure 18.2) is based on the same idea as Japanese candlestick charts, which place special emphasis on the relationship of the opening price and the closing price.[1] This is a very important concept—so important that EquityTrader.com's price bars were designed as a kind of Western candlestick, with the portion between the open and close green if the close is higher than the open or red if the close is lower, and with the balance of the range in dark blue.

The underlying idea is that when a stock is really strong, it will trade higher after the opening, no matter how strong the opening;

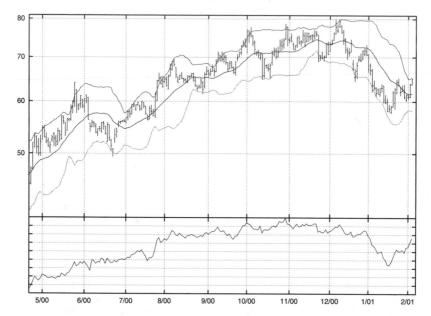

Figure 18.2   Accumulation Distribution, Hartford Insurance, 200 days.
AD diagnoses this top just as well as Intraday Intensity.

weakness is indicated if the market cannot trade higher into the
close. Likewise a weak opening followed by further weakness is a
continuing negative, while a weak opening followed by strength is
positive.

Candlestick charting is hundreds of years old, and the
Japanese have learned to focus heavily on the patterns formed
by the candles, especially certain groupings of candles. We find it
interesting to use the candles themselves to add some extra visual
value to Western-style charts by elucidating the price action as
only candles can do—especially price action near the Bollinger
Bands. For example, a transition from red bodies—where the close
is lower than the open—to green bodies—where the close is higher
than the open—near the lower band is an indication of a bottom.
That transition would be mirrored in Accumulation Distribution,
especially if volume rose with the turn in the tide.

Both Intraday Intensity and Accumulation Distribution can be
presented in open-ended form by keeping a cumulative sum from
the first calculation point of the individual-period readings and
plotting the result as a line. They also can be presented in the form

Table 18.4 Formula for Normalizing Volume Oscillators

10-day sum of [(close − open)/(high − low) ∗ volume]/
                                  10-day sum of volume

of an oscillator by keeping an *n*-period moving sum of the periodic readings, where *n* is typically 10 or 20 periods. Some people find it easier to read the unbounded indicator line; some people prefer the oscillator format. For comparison to trading bands, the oscillator format seems easier to interpret for most.

Either an II or AD oscillator can be normalized so that it is directly comparable from issue to issue by dividing it by the total volume over the calculation period. Table 18.4 presents the formula for a 10-day normalized Accumulation Distribution oscillator, and Figure 18.3 presents the result. The normalized versions are often referred to as percents, i.e., 21-day II% or 10-day AD%.

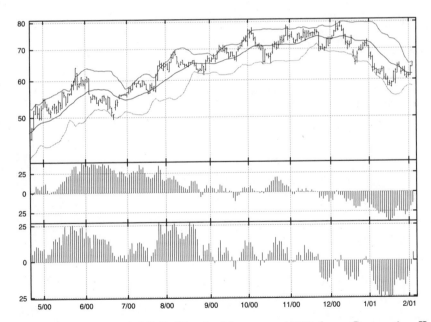

Figure 18.3 II% and AD%, Hartford Insurance, 200 days. Converting II and AD to oscillators often uncovers data that is hard to see otherwise.

In the fourth category we find the Money Flow Index, which elegantly imbues Welles Wilder's Relative Strength Index concept with volume data. At the core of the RSI calculation is a ratio of two exponential averages, one of the changes on up periods and another of the changes on down periods. MFI replaces those exponential averages with moving sums of price times volume, one of positive days and one of negative days. Common sum lengths are 9 for short-term purposes and 14 as recommended by Wilder in his original presentation.

With MFI you are asking the question, does the volume differential between up days and down days confirm the momentum of the trend? A rally with strong volume on the up days and contracting volume on the down days will produce a stronger MFI than would an RSI of the same period.

MFI turns out to be a bit more volatile than RSI. It does not trend as smoothly, and it exhibits a greater range. Therefore we use the levels of 80 and 20 as MFI benchmarks rather than the standard benchmark levels of 70 and 30 used for RSI. This results in roughly equivalent signals (Figure 18.4).

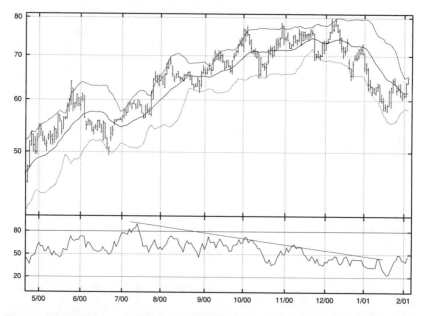

Figure 18.4 Money Flow Index, Hartford Insurance, 200 days. Note the steadily deteriorating trend in MFI as the rally matures.

Our second indicator from the fourth category is Volume-Weighted MACD. MACD is Gerald Appel's Moving Average Convergence/Divergence. To our mind, MACD is primarily a trend indicator. It consists of two lines, MACD itself and the signal line. MACD is the difference between two averages, widely known as a departure chart. The signal line is an exponential average of MACD.[2]

To volume-weight MACD you substitute volume-weighted moving averages[3] for the exponential averages used in MACD (Figure 18.5). The signal line alone remains an exponential average. Like MFI, VWMACD is a bit more sensitive than its parent, but it doesn't require any adjustment of its parameters for successful use.

When volume-weighting MACD, you are asking the question, Does volume support the trend? If it does, then VWMACD will be strong. If it doesn't, VWMACD will nicely highlight the underlying weakness. This concept seems especially important

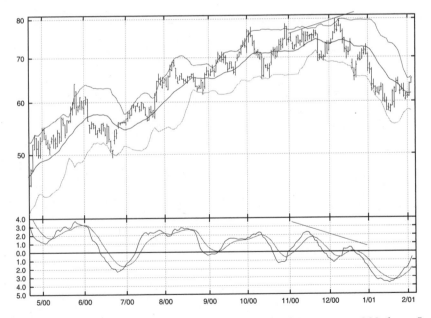

Figure 18.5 Volume-Weighted MACD, Hartford Insurance, 200 days. It is possible to construct successful timing systems based on volume-weighted MACD alone.

when institutional trading is the real driving force behind the market.

In this chapter we have presented four volume indicators. To some extent they are noncorrelated. While Accumulation Distribution and Intraday Intensity are both derived from a single period's data, they use very different calculations and variables. MFI is really a volume-imbued momentum indicator, while VWMACD is a volume-weighted trend indicator. Where these indicators agree, they can be treated as one. Where they disagree, one must focus on the story that each tells in relation to its methodology and ferret out the truth.

For a more in-depth discussion of volume indicators, please see my paper "Volume Indicators" (see the Bibliography).

Now we turn to the next two chapters for a couple of practical applications.

KEY POINTS TO REMEMBER

- Volume is an independent variable.
- Volume indicators may be categorized by calculation type.
- Focus on AD, II, MFI, and VWMACD.
- Look at both open and closed forms of AD and II.

19

METHOD II: TREND FOLLOWING

Method II anticipates the birth of trends by looking at strength in price confirmed by indicator strength. The idea is that when price is sufficiently strong to approach the upper band, and that strength is echoed by strength in an appropriate indicator, we may anticipate the beginning of an uptrend (Figure 19.1). Of course, the opposite is true as well (Figure 19.2). In essence, this is a variation on Method I, with the indicator MFI being used for confirmation and no requirement for a Squeeze. This method may anticipate some Method I signals.

We'll use the same exit techniques, a modified version of Parabolic or a tag of the Bollinger Band on the opposite side of the trade. The idea is that both %b for price and MFI must rise above our threshold. The basic rule is, if %b is greater than 0.8 and MFI(10) is greater than 80, then buy.

Recall that %b shows us where we are within the bands; at 1 we are at the upper band, and at 0 we are at the lower band.

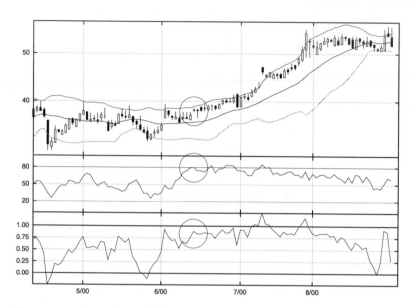

Figure 19.1   Method II buy example, AG Edwards, 100 days. Strong price action plus strong indicator action equals a buy signal.

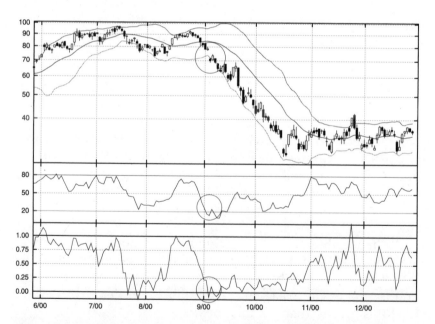

Figure 19.2   Method II sell example, Micron, 150 days. Weakness in price confirmed by weakness in MFI equals a sell signal.

So at 0.8, %b is telling us that we are 80 percent of the way up from the lower band to the upper band. Another way of looking at that is that we are in the top 20 percent of the area between the bands. MFI is a bounded indicator running between 0 and 100. Thus, 80 is a very strong reading representing the upper trigger level, similar in significance to 70 for RSI.

So Method II combines price strength with indicator strength to forecast higher prices, or price weakness with indicator weakness to forecast lower prices.

We'll use the basic Bollinger Band settings of 20 periods and ± 2 standard deviations. To set the MFI parameters we'll employ an old rule: Indicator length should be approximately half the length of the calculation period for the bands. Though the exact origin of this rule is unknown to me, it is likely an adaptation of a rule from cycle analysis that suggests using moving averages a quarter the length of the dominant cycle. Experimentation showed that periods a quarter of the calculation period for the bands were generally too short, but that a half-length period for the indicators worked quite well. As with all things, these are but starting values. This approach offers many variations you can explore, as shown in Table 19.1. Also, any of the inputs could be varied as a function of the characteristics of the vehicle being traded to create a more adaptive system.

The main trap to avoid is late entry, since much of the potential may have been used up. A problem with Method II is that the risk-reward characteristics are harder to quantify, as the move may

Table 19.1   Method II Variations

Volume-Weighted MACD could be substituted for MFI.*

The strength (threshold) required for both %b and the indicator can be varied.

The speed of the Parabolic also can be varied.

The length parameter for the Bollinger Bands could be adjusted.†

---

*A variation on VWMACD, VWMACD histogram, would be a very good choice if VWMACD were a bit too slow in your application. It is the difference between VWMACD and its signal line (the nine-day average of VWMACD). It is a shorter-term, more sensitive indicator than VWMACD. The same procedure can be done on MACD itself. The result is called a MACD histogram and is quite a popular technique.

†Adjusting %b is the same as adjusting the BandWidth parameter.

have been under way for a bit before the signal is issued. One approach to avoiding this trap is to wait for a pullback after the signal and then buy the first up day. This will miss some setups, but those remaining will have better risk-reward ratios.

It would be best to test this approach on the types of stocks you actually trade or want to trade, and set the parameters according to the characteristics of those stocks and your own risk-reward criteria. For example, if you traded very volatile growth stocks, you might look at higher levels for the %b (greater than 1 is a possibility), MFI, and Parabolic parameters. Higher levels of all three would pick stronger stocks and accelerate the stops more quickly.[1] More risk-averse investors should focus on high Parabolic parameters, while more patient investors anxious to give these trades more time to work out should focus on smaller Parabolic constants, which result in the stop-out level rising more slowly.

A very interesting adjustment is to start the Parabolic not under the entry day as is common, but under the most recent significant low or turning point. For example, in buying a bottom, the Parabolic could be started under the low rather than on the entry day. This has the distinct advantage of capturing the character of the most recent trading. Using the opposite band as an exit allows these trades to develop the most, but it may leave the stop uncomfortably far away for some.

This is worth reiterating: Another variation of this approach is to use these signals as alerts and trade the first pullback after the alert is given (Figure 19.3). This approach will reduce the number of trades—some trades will be missed, but it will also reduce the number of whipsaws. In essence, this is quite a robust method that should be adaptable to a wide variety of trading styles and temperaments.

There is one other idea here that can be important: Rational Analysis. This method buys confirmed strength and sells confirmed weakness. So wouldn't it be a good idea to presort our universe of candidates by fundamental criteria, creating buy lists and sell lists? Then take only buy signals for the stocks on the buy list and sell signals for the stocks on the sell list. Such filtering is beyond the scope of this book, but Rational Analysis, the juncture of the sets of fundamental and technical analysis, offers a robust approach to the problems most investors face. Prescreening

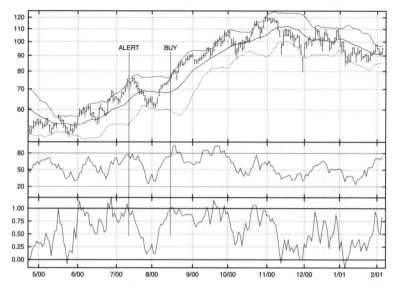

Figure 19.3 Method II as an alert, PerkinElmer, 200 days. Near misses on the part of our methodology should be seen as alerts.

for desirable fundamental candidates or problematic stocks is sure to improve your results.

Another approach to filtering signals is to look at the EquityTrader.com performance ratings and take buys on stocks rated 1 or 2 and sell on stocks rated 4 or 5. These are front-weighted, risk-adjusted performance ratings that can be thought of as relative strength compensated for downside volatility.

KEY POINTS TO REMEMBER

- Method II buys strength and sells weakness.
- Buy when %b is greater than 0.8 and MFI is greater than 80.
- Sell when %b is less than 0.2 and MFI is less than 20.
- Use a Parabolic stop.
- May anticipate Method I.
- Explore the variations.
- Use Rational Analysis.
- Lists of Method II candidates are available on www.BollingeronBollingerBands.com.

C H A P T E R

20

METHOD III:
REVERSALS

Method III anticipates reversals by comparing tags of the bands to indicator action. Initially we look at multiple upper-band tags accompanied by deteriorating indicators and multiple lower-band tags accompanied by strengthening indicators. Then we look at tags in isolation where the indicators are in the opposite state—a lower band tag with a positive indicator or an upper band tag with a negative indicator.

Somewhere in the early 1970s the idea of shifting a moving average up and down by a fixed percentage to form an envelope around the price structure caught on. All you had to do was multiply the average by 1 plus the desired percent to get the upper band, or divide by 1 plus the desired percent to get the lower band, which was a computationally easy idea at a time when computation was either time-consuming or costly. This was the day of columnar pads, adding machines and pencils, and, for the lucky, mechanical calculators.

Naturally market timers and stock pickers quickly took up the idea, as it gave them access to definitions of high and low they could use in their timing operations. Oscillators were very much in vogue at the time, and this led to a number of systems comparing the action of price within percentage bands with oscillator action. Perhaps the best known at the time—and still widely used today—was a system that compared the action of the Dow Jones Industrial Average within bands created by shifting its 21-day moving average up and down 4 percent with one of two oscillators based on broad market trading statistics. The first was a 21-day sum of advancing minus declining issues on the NYSE. The second, also from the NYSE, was a 21-day sum of up volume minus down volume. Tags of the upper band accompanied by negative oscillator readings from either oscillator were taken as sell signals. Buy signals were generated by tags of the lower band accompanied by positive oscillator readings from either oscillator. Coincident readings from both oscillators served to increase confidence. For stocks for which broad market data wasn't available, a volume indicator such as a 21-day version Bostian's Intraday Intensity was used. This approach and a myriad of variants remain in use today as useful timing guides.

Many modifications to this approach are possible, and many have been made. My own contribution was to substitute a departure graph for the 21-day summing technique used for the oscillators. A departure graph is a graph of the difference of two averages, a short-term average and a long-term average. In this case, the averages are of daily advances minus declines and daily up volume minus down volume, and the periods to use for the averages are 21 and 100. The plot is of the short-term average minus the long-term average.

The prime benefit of using the departure technique to create the oscillators is that the use of the long-term moving average has the effect of adjusting (normalizing) for long-term biases in market structure.[1] Without this adjustment, a simple advance-decline (A-D) oscillator (Figure 20.1) or up-volume–down-volume oscillator will likely fool you from time to time. However, using the difference between averages very nicely adjusts for the bullish or bearish biases that cause the problem.

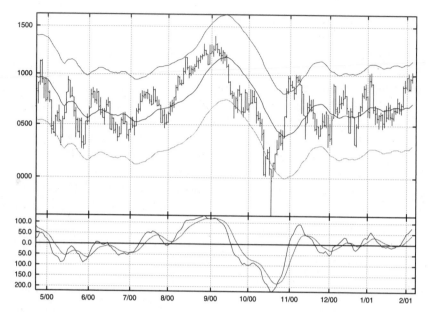

Figure 20.1 DJIA with 4 percent bands and advance-decline oscillator. MACD is used to create an advance-decline oscillator for timing with percentage bands.

Choosing the departure technique also means that you can use the widely available MACD calculations to create the oscillators (Figure 20.2). Set the first MACD parameter to 21, the second to 100, and the third to 9. This sets the period for the short-term average to 21 days, sets the period for the long-term average to 100 days, and leaves the period for the signal line at the default, 9 days. The data inputs are advances-declines and up volume–down volume. If the program you are using wants the inputs in percentages, the first should be 9 percent, the second 2 percent, and the third 20 percent.[2] Now substitute Bollinger Bands[3] for the percentage bands and you have the core of a very useful reversal system for timing markets.

In a similar vein we can use indicators to clarify tops and bottoms and confirm reversals in trend. To wit, if we form a W2 bottom with %b higher on the retest than on the initial low—a relative W4 (Figure 20.3)—check your volume oscillator, either MFI or VWMACD, to see if it has a similar pattern.[4] If it does, then buy the first strong up day; if it doesn't, wait and look for another setup.

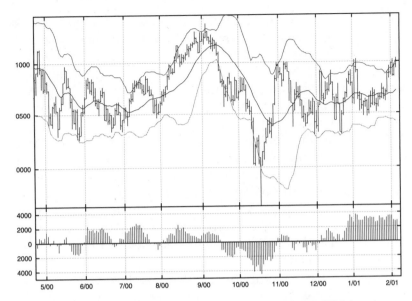

Figure 20.2   DJIA with Bollinger Bands and A-D MACD histogram, the difference between the two MACD lines from Figure 20.1.

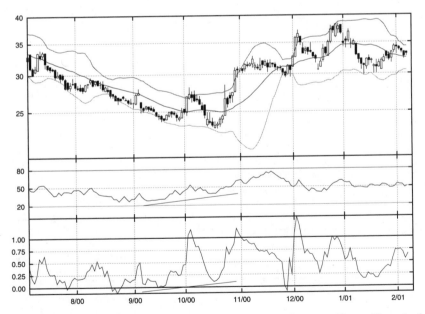

Figure 20.3   W2 (W4) with Accumulation Distribution, Dow Chemical, 150 days. AD confirms price action as depicted by %b.

The logic at tops is similar, but we need to be more patient. As is typical, the top takes longer and usually presents the classic three or more pushes to a high. In a classic formation, %b will be lower on each push, as will a volume indicator such as Accumulation Distribution (Figure 20.4). After such a pattern develops, look at selling meaningful down days where volume and range are greater than average.

What we are doing in Method III is clarifying tops and bottoms by involving an independent variable, volume, in our analysis via the use of volume indicators to help get a better picture of the shifting nature of supply and demand. Is demand increasing across a W bottom? If so, we ought to be interested in buying. Is supply increasing each time we make a new push to a high? If so, we ought to be marshaling our defenses or thinking about shorting if so inclined.

Method III can be simplified and systematized quite easily. Instead of looking for a steady deterioration as the pattern develops, we can look for discrete opportunities. The best way to do this is to find tags of the bands where an oscillator such as a

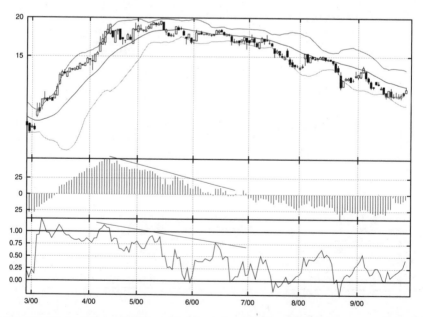

Figure 20.4 M16 (M12) with Accumulation Distribution, Lyondell, 150 days. Steadily waning %b and A-D portray a top.

21-day II% or 20-day AD% is opposite to the tag—a tag of the upper band accompanied by a negative indicator reading or a tag of the lower band accompanied by a positive indicator reading. Now, this approach can be systematized. For example, go long if %b is less than 0.05 and II% is greater than zero. Or go short if %b is greater than 0.95 and AD% is less than zero.

These positive-tag/negative indicator and negative-tag/positive indicator setups are actually where I got on the bus, and remain near and dear to me. Indeed, I bought a Method III setup with a close outside the band right at long-term support that couldn't have been diagnosed any other way. It was a scary place on the chart, a triple bottom and a potential breakdown. But II% was very positive, and there was a strong up day the day after the low, clearly suggesting a completed setup. Most importantly, a new low for the stock was close by the entry point, so my risk was well defined, about 2½ points. A tag of the upper band, the logical target after such a setup, was 10 points away, suggesting a risk-reward ratio of near 4 to 1. Not too shabby!

It is this ability to deliver setups with good risk-reward ratios that most highly commends Method III setups. The bottom line here is clarification of patterns which are potentially interesting, but on which you might not have the confidence to act without corroboration.

KEY POINTS TO REMEMBER

- The buy setup: lower band tag and the oscillator positive.
- The sell setup: upper band tag and oscillator negative.
- Use MACD to calculate the breadth indicators.
- Lists of Method III candidates are available on www.BollingeronBollingerBands.com.

PART

V

ADVANCED TOPICS

Part V presents the advanced topics of day trading and using Bollinger Bands to normalize indicators. Chart types, indicators, and techniques for day traders are reviewed, and the power technique of using Bollinger Bands to normalize indicators is presented.

21

NORMALIZING
INDICATORS

Bollinger Bands need not be confined to use on security or index prices. To name just a few of the possibilities, they can be used on ratios, economic series, fundamental data, volume, and technical indicators. It doesn't matter whether these series are presented as oscillators or as series without bounds. In each case Bollinger Bands serve the same function they serve with price; they define high or low on a relative basis. This can often add great insight that the traditional rigid levels and rules can't deliver.

Take the Relative Strength Index, RSI, as an example. The traditional rules call for an overbought interpretation when the indicator rises above 70 and an oversold interpretation when the indicator falls below 30. Perhaps the most commonly employed technique using this indicator is to buy a positive crossing of 30 and sell a negative crossing of 70. This, however, can be problematic. Sometimes 70 and 30 work, sometimes they don't, and sometimes they fail spectacularly.

For a more robust approach to RSI, take the observation that in a prolonged bull run the 70-30 decision frame rises, with some analysts recommending 80 and 40 as the benchmarks, and that in a prolonged downturn the frame falls, with 60 and 20 being recommended benchmarks. Indeed, a tag of 80 can be used to define an uptrend, with 40 being used thereafter as oversold until a tag of 20 reverses the structure and suggests a new downtrend, with 60 now being overbought. Thus the action of the RSI indicator can be used both to define the major trend of the market and to shift the decision frames to the appropriate levels to identify overbought-oversold relative to trend.[1]

A bit of a digression is in order. In the old days, *overbought* and *oversold* were terms used to denote climactic conditions. In the fall of 1974, at the end of the last great bear market, the stock market was oversold; and in the spring of 1962, as the bowling stock craze[2] crested, the stock market was overbought. Analysts looked for these phenomena to occur infrequently and to mark important long-term turning points in the markets. The passing years have seen the relentless contraction of the time frame; these definitions have become moot for the typical investor. Today *overbought* and *oversold* are applied to the very shortest of time frames, a practice that no doubt earlier analysts would find simply incredible. However, we must accept the basic definition as applicable to all time frames: to have come too far, too fast.

While the shifting of the decision frame for RSI according to market conditions is a clear improvement over the simple 30-70 interpretation, we can do better still. How? By plotting Bollinger Bands on the indicator and using the bands to set the overbought and oversold levels. By using Bollinger Bands in this manner, we obtain a fully adaptive approach that morphs with the market. First a bit on setting up Bollinger Bands on indicators; then a neat trick.

Indicators are a more diverse lot than stocks. Unlike stocks where 20 periods and 2 standard deviations are the best departure points for the vast majority of issues, each indicator seems to require its own parameters (see Table 21.1). In general, the appropriate averages tend to run longer than those for stocks, a fact already acknowledged in our use of a 50-day average for volume. Other than that, no general guidance is possible due to variation in indicator parameters and formulations. However, an example of a setup that works quite well is a 14-day RSI with 50-day, 2.1-standard deviation Bollinger Bands. Using this combination of parameters, overbought and oversold levels for most stocks are easily identified, and clear divergences are delineated at many turning points.

A sharp eye will soon hone in on the appropriate Bollinger Band parameters for any indicator application. Start with the same average-length-picking approach that was discussed earlier for stocks. What you want to see is a slow transition in which the average lives in the upper range of the indicator during uptrends and in the lower range during downtrends. However, the average should stay in the middle portion of the chart, for MFI roughly between 25 and 75, and for RSI a bit tighter, between 30 and 70. If the average gets into the upper quarter or lower quarter of the range, you have an average that is too short. If the average barely budges from the midpoint, you have an average that is too long. Then set the number of standard deviations for the bands, starting with 2, so that between 85 and 90 percent of all observations fall within the bands.

There is a reason that these indicator parameters vary greatly; indicators tend to be distributed in quite a different manner than stocks. In fact, some indicators are distributed in a decidedly non-normal fashion. Stochastics tends to have fat tails and can even have a U-shaped distribution where the tails are fatter than the middle (Figure 21.1), while RSI tends to have thinner tails. However, you need not concern yourself with the statistics. If you follow the above procedure, you'll end up with a workable approach.

Table 21.1 Trial Bollinger Band Values for Indicators

Indicator	Length	Width
9-period RSI	40	2.0
14-period RSI	50	2.1
10-period MFI	40	2.0
21-period II	40	2.0

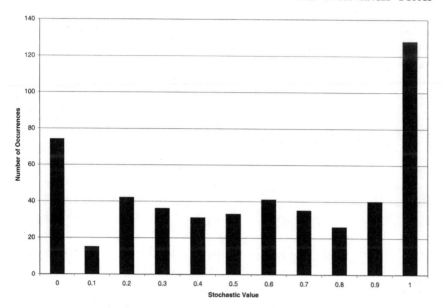

Figure 21.1 Distribution chart, 10-day stochastic, IBM, two years. This is about as far from a normal distribution as you can get.

Now, treat the upper band as you would an overbought level; for example, 70 for the Relative Strength Index. And treat the lower band as an oversold level; for example, 20 for the Money Flow Index. If you have set the correct parameters, all the regular decision rules will hold, such as buying a positive crossing of the lower band or treating a tag of the upper band as an overbought signal. There is no need to worry about rigid frames or rules any more; they have been made moot. Trade in sync with the prevailing trends using the indicators within the bands as your guide to opportunities.

And now for our neat trick. If you will, a bit of indicator magic: %b is normally used to depict the location of a data point, typically the close or last, within the Bollinger Bands. At 1.0 we are at the upper band, at 0.5 we are at the middle band, and at 0.0 we are at the lower band. The range of %b is not confined to the zero-to-1 interval. A reading of 1.1 tells us we are 10 percent of the BandWidth above the upper band, and a reading of −0.15 says we are 15 percent below the lower band using BandWidth as a gauge. First, calculate and plot your indicator. Second, plot Bollinger Bands on it using the method just described to set the parameters.

Table 21.2 Normalized Indicator Formula

(Indicator − indicator lower band)/(indicator upper band − indicator lower band)

Third, calculate %b (see Table 21.2) using the indicator and the bands just plotted. Fourth, plot %b alone as a normalized version of the indicator! Ta-da! See Figures 21.2 and 21.3 for examples using MFI.

What we have done is redrawn the indicator using the upper and lower bands as the boundaries instead of the absolute possible range of the indicator—0 to 100 in the case of RSI. This normalization of indicators is one of the most important uses of the %b formula. To refer to an indicator normalized in this fashion, we write %b(RSI) (see Figures 21.4 and 21.5).

Normalization of an indicator using Bollinger Bands allows the indicator to be included in trading systems in an adaptive manner. The technique can be applied to open-ended indicators that

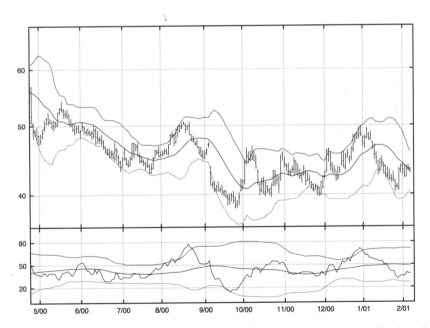

Figure 21.2 MFI with Bollinger Bands, Dupont, 150 days. The bands define high and low rather than the rigid 20 and 80 levels typically used.

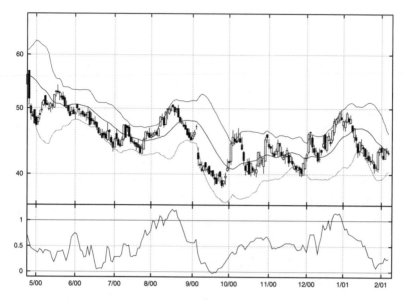

Figure 21.3 %b(MFI), Dupont, 150 days. Overbought and oversold are defined far more clearly.

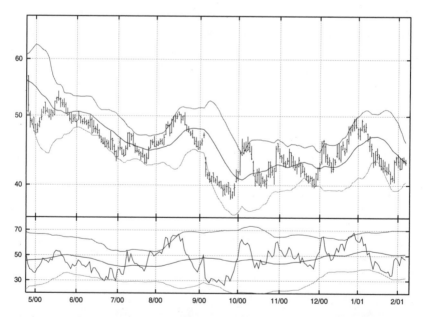

Figure 21.4 RSI with Bollinger Bands, Dupont, 150 days. Note how well the bands work as definitions of overbought and oversold.

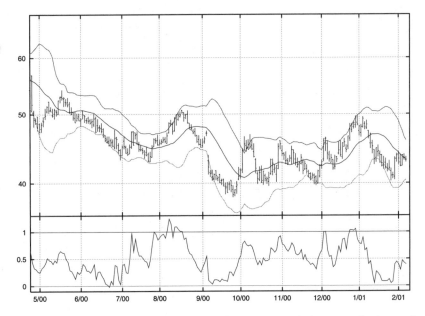

Figure 21.5 %b(RSI), Dupont, 150 days. A much-improved view of indicator action.

are formed by taking continuous sums of the daily readings, or oscillators that swing back and forth within a predetermined range or above and below a centerline. In either case, the new definitions of high and low afforded by this method allow the user to integrate the information from the indicator into a rigorous trading process in an adaptive manner unobtainable before.

KEY POINTS TO REMEMBER

- Use Bollinger Bands to normalize indicator levels.
- Generally, longer average lengths are needed.
- Try replotting the indicator as %b.

22

DAY TRADING

Bollinger Bands are widely used in the daytrading community. They are used on everything from tick charts on up, and they are used in many different ways. Indicators, when used with the bands, tend to be trend or momentum indicators. Volume indicators are an interesting alternative, though day traders rarely use them.

The most critical part of day trading is chart selection. The finest gradation is the tick chart. Most traders will want to keep a tick chart going for their short-term reference. This chart should have the bid and ask plotted along with the ticks for the last sale— although plotting the bid and ask may cause the chart to become too cluttered for really active stocks. Connecting the ticks is a nicety that can get you into trouble, as it encourages a belief in greater continuity than may actually be exhibited by the price structure. A time frame of a day or two is usually fine, but you may find that the charts of very active stocks are too densely packed with information for even a day to be useful. If that is the case, you may need to utilize a shorter span for readability, perhaps half a day.

You will need to find out what the normal trading hours are for what you are analyzing; your trading desk will know. Then set those hours as the defaults for your charts. They can be changed later if something extraordinary happens—an after-hours blowup or some such—but in the meantime you'll eliminate the dead space between sessions and facilitate analytical continuity from session to session. This is especially important if you are going to try to have indicators span sessions.

When it comes to chart analysis, bar charts and candlesticks rule. For the short term you'll need the shortest interval that produces robust bars. The easiest way to quantify robustness for a bar is to look at the last price of each bar. If the last equals the high or the low a preponderance of the time, the bar length for that stock is too short (Figure 22.1). Lengthen the time frame for the bars slowly until you start to get properly formed bars

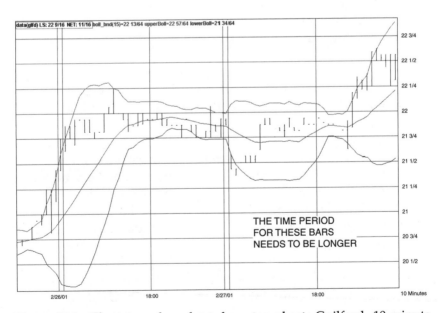

Figure 22.1 Short-term bar chart, bars too short, Guilford, 10-minute bars. Too short a time frame; collapsed bars; too many closes at high or low of bar; little price development; prolonged Squeeze.

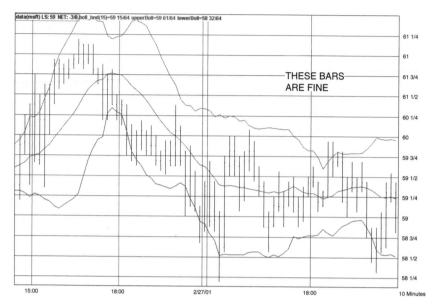

Figure 22.2 Short-term bar chart, bars correct, Microsoft, 10-minute bars. A much better depiction of price action.

(Figure 22.2), not just lines with the last rattling back and forth between the high and the low. The goal is to get a view of the price formation mechanism at work, not just a record of the back and forth between the bid and ask price. Once you know what the best time period for your short-term bars is, you can select a couple of longer-term charts to serve in the intermediate and long-term roles.

    If you can find intervals both for your bars and for your charts that make sense within the context of the market, you'll be much better off. Days, weeks, months, and quarters were "gimmes" that no one had to think about, but how do you divide a day up sensibly? Start with hours—treating the first half hour as a full hour. That renders a seven-hour day on the chart. Consider including the preopening session as an hour and postclose trading as another hour. With that method, each day would have nine hours. Or try my favorite—half hours, with presession and postsession trading allocated one period each. That makes for 15 bars per day.

    You'll want intervals that make psychological sense for your charts, intervals that others are looking at or are at least aware of, intervals that fit the natural rhythms of trading as closely as possible. Otherwise the information content will be lost. Of course, you'll need to consider what suits your style and what is appropriate for your trading vehicles. But whatever you do, try to fit your charts to the reality of the marketplace as well as you can without compromising your style.[1]

Now, armed with a basic set of charts, it is time to consider which analytical techniques to deploy. Bollinger Bands and the related techniques discussed in this book are widely used in day trading, and much of the material discussed earlier is directly applicable. In chatting with day traders, I've found two common themes, selling and buying the extremes and trading volatility breakouts. Both of these approaches are well suited to Bollinger Bands.

Let's review a bit. Bruce Babcock, the late publisher of *Commodity Trader's Consumer Report*, said his favorite approach to trading was the use of a volatility-breakout system. This kind of system has much in common with Bollinger Bands. (The use of Bollinger Bands to construct a volatility-breakout system was discussed in Chapters 15 and 16.) Typically, the average is shortened and the bands are tightened. Then when a Squeeze occurs and the upper band is exceeded, a buy signal is triggered. Generally, some stop such as a Parabolic is used for the exit. Falling back inside the bands can also be used as an exit signal. The opposite logic is true as well. A short sale signal is triggered by falling below the lower band after a Squeeze. Again a stop system such as reentering the bands or a parabolic is used. Be very careful about using breakout logic in the absence of a Squeeze. In our experience The Squeeze is a necessary element of the approach.

When it comes to transacting at the extremes, in day trading Bollinger Bands can be used as references for overbought and oversold. Rallies that carry far above the upper band can be sold at the first sign of weakness, with the immediately prior high as a stop and vice versa. And the bands themselves give signals, as in the case of the lower bands turning up after a breakaway trend to give an end-of-trend signal. Also, if the band parameters are well matched to the security being traded, then failures at the bands can be treated as entry points with an initial price target of the middle band.

Volume indicators can be very useful in day trading, but they also can be problematic due to the uneven distribution of volume during the day. Typically most of the volume is transacted near the beginning and end of the day.[2] Try the volume indicators presented in this book on the charts you trade to see which work best in your environment. AD and II will only work well if your bars are very well specified—that is, if they reflect the underlying trading mechanisms well. You'll stand a better chance with MFI and VWMACD.

Pay close attention to the splits between trading sessions, especially if you have set up your charts so one session abuts the next. If gaps occur, be extra careful. The price-formation mechanism continues on, even when the official market is closed. New information is discovered and may be reflected on other exchanges, or in after-hour or preopen sessions, or in price gaps between the prior session's close and the next day's open. This "outside" information can distort averages, bands, and indicators alike.

Really with slight variations, just about all of the basic Bollinger Band techniques and uses are applicable to short-term trading. It is just a matter of suiting the approach to your style and choosing the charting period well.

KEY POINTS TO REMEMBER

- Choose your charts carefully.
- Tighten BB parameters for trading breakouts after Squeezes.
- Sell reversals outside the bands.
- Try volume indicators.
- Be careful about crossing session boundaries.

P A R T

VI

SUMMING UP

Part VI wraps things up. First there is a list of 15 basic rules to use when employing Bollinger Bands and then some closing comments.

Following Part VI are three important sections: the Endnotes, the Glossary, and the Bibliography. The Endnotes contain related thoughts that just didn't quite fit in the main text, the Glossary defines all our terms, and the Bibliography is a rich source of ideas for further reading.

Finally, bound inside the back cover is a reference card with the 15 rules, the M and W patterns, and the key parameters and formulas.

15 BASIC RULES

In closing, here are 15 basic rules to remember regarding Bollinger Bands:

1. Bollinger Bands provide a relative definition of high and low.
2. That relative definition can be used to compare price action and indicator action to arrive at rigorous buy and sell decisions.
3. Appropriate indicators can be derived from momentum, volume, sentiment, open interest, intermarket data, etc.
4. Volatility and trend already have been deployed in the construction of Bollinger Bands, so their use for confirmation of price action is not recommended.
5. The indicators used for confirmation should not be directly related to one another. Two indicators from the same category do not increase confirmation. Avoid collinearity.

6. Bollinger Bands can be used to clarify pure price patterns such as M-type tops and W-type bottoms, momentum shifts, etc.

7. Price can, and does, walk up the upper Bollinger Band and down the lower Bollinger Band.

8. Closes outside the Bollinger Bands can be continuation signals, not reversal signals—as is demonstrated by the use of Bollinger Bands in some very successful volatility-break-out systems.

9. The default parameter of 20 periods for calculating the moving average and standard deviation and the default parameter of 2 standard deviations for the BandWidth are just that, defaults. The actual parameters needed for any given market or task may be different.

10. The average deployed should not be the best one for crossover signals. Rather, it should be descriptive of the intermediate-term trend.

11. If the average is lengthened, the number of standard deviations needs to be increased simultaneously—from 2 at 20 periods to 2.1 at 50 periods. Likewise, if the average is shortened, the number of standard deviations should be reduced—from 2 at 20 periods to 1.9 at 10 periods.

12. Bollinger Bands are based upon a simple moving average. This is because a simple moving average is used in the standard deviation calculation and we wish to be logically consistent.

13. Be careful about making statistical assumptions based on the use of the standard deviation calculation in the construction of the bands. The sample size in most deployments of Bollinger Bands is too small for statistical significance, and the distributions involved are rarely normal.

14. Indicators can be normalized with %b, eliminating fixed thresholds in the process.

15. Finally, tags of the bands are just that—tags, not signals. A tag of the upper Bollinger Band is *not* in and of itself a sell signal. A tag of the lower Bollinger Band is *not* in and of itself a buy signal.

WRAPPING IT UP

This book opened with a discussion of relativity, so it is only fitting that we return to relativity in the end. Oliver Wendell Holmes, Jr., believed that jurisprudence must adapt to the times, and he fought against judges bringing their own beliefs to bear on their cases. In this regard Holmes can be seen as a prototype for the enlightened investor. He weighed matters in a context that was relative to the case, to the law, and to society. He did not let his emotions carry him along, nor did he let his personal beliefs blur his decisions. In addition, he was dead set against judges making the law. These principles—relativity, discipline, and judicial restraint—are directly applicable to investing. To be a Holmeslike investor, test your beliefs to see whether they are true, make your decisions in a relative framework, do so without letting your emotions color the process, and do not change the rules as you go.

This book presents a relative decision framework that is fully adaptive. It should stand you in good stead for many years to come. Markets do change, as do economies, investors, and all the rest. However, these tools should morph with the markets, driven, as they are, by market variables, price, volatility, and volume.

The music critic Scott Yanow, in his *All Music Guide to Jazz*, (published by Miller Freeman Books), described musician Albert Ayler this way:

> *It could be said of tenor-saxophonist Albert Ayler whose music advanced from screaming sound explorations to early New Orleans-type marching bands, [that he] went so far ahead that he eventually came in at the beginning!*

Bollinger Bands and their related tools and techniques are sufficiently advanced that their use should allow you to concentrate on the real matters at hand, trading and investing. In essence, by employing these tools you are free to get back to basics. It is up to you to decide whether I have followed in Albert Ayler's footsteps. I hope I have.

One of the great joys of having invented an analytical technique such as Bollinger Bands is seeing what other people do with it. There are many ways to use Bollinger Bands, and I invite you to explore various techniques in your own analysis. Please let me know of any discoveries you make or innovations you achieve. I can be reached via e-mail at BBands@BollingerBands.com.

Last, but not least, I am always asked how to prepare for investing. First, a college-level statistics course of the type given in the psychology department will provide you with the foundation you need to understand the numbers you are working with. Second, a few basic psychology courses will shed some light on the workings of the market, especially if one of them is a course in mass psychology. Finally, learn how to program. BASIC is a good place to start, as is LISP. Although C has become the language of choice for serious developers, BASIC will be sufficient to let you deal with the analysis programs you are most likely to run into. And while LISP may not be the language de jour, mastering it can be fun and will give you a set of skills you will find useful no matter what language you settle into. Whatever you do, don't let computers intimidate you. They are just tools, and can be fun and rewarding to explore.

Investing is a tough task; take care out there.

ENDNOTES

Preface

1. Over the years, large portions of what was once regarded as technical analysis have been carved off and included in the quantitative and behavioral disciplines. Today, quantitative analysis, largely a blend of technical and fundamental concepts, has a large institutional following. Behavioralists are largely confined to academia at present, but are starting to make inroads among serious investors. While categories are confusing, the concept behind Rational Analysis is not; take what works without regard for labels and use it.

Chapter 1

1. Michael White and John Gribbin, *Einstein: A Life in Science*, New York: Dutton Books, 1994.

2. Oliver Wendell Holmes, Jr., *The Common Law,* Boston: Little, Brown & Co., 1881; reprinted by Dover Publications, Boston, 1991.

Chapter 2

1. Line charts can give a false sense of continuity by connecting points for which there is no logical connection. Continuity implied by connecting the dots can also be a problem for indicators and other nonprice series where the data points are independent of one another.
2. Actually some point-and-figure charts can include a reference to time. For example, for daily charts the first posting each month, whether an X or an O, can be replaced by the number of that month, 1 for January, 11 for November, etc. Similar schemes can be employed for other time frames.
3. The 50-day average is the most commonly used average for this purpose, and for most traders this should work well. However, feel free to lengthen it or shorten it to fit your trading style.

Chapter 3

1. Another starting point for determining the calculation length for Bollinger Bands is to run a moving-average crossover optimization. With this technical procedure, you select the moving average that produces the best buy and sell signals when it is crossed by price. Double the length of the optimization results. This will often put you in the right ballpark and can be used as a check for the visual method. The logic behind this arises from cycle analysis, where quarter- and half-cycle moving averages often produce useful results.
2. Insensitivity to small changes in parameters is a key criterion in developing trading systems. For example, a system that produces similar results with 18-, 20-, and 22-period averages is far superior to a system that produces great results at 20 periods, but so-so results at 18 and 22 periods.

Chapter 4

1. See Garfield Drew, *New Methods for Profit in the Stock Market*, 1955, reprinted by Fraser Books, Burlington, Vt., for a discussion of some famous investment plans.

2. Certain highly adaptive systems may be exempt from this dictum, at least to some extent. Fuzzy logic, neural networks, and genetic algorithms are tools that may well allow a system to be adaptive enough to survive. See www.EquityTrader.com for an example.

Chapter 5

1. Eventually broad concepts may achieve such widespread acceptance that they become diluted or perhaps even inverted in extreme cases. Witness the expected long-term outperformance of small-capitalization stocks, a concept that became so widely embraced it vanished completely. In the parlance it is said that it was "arbitraged out of existence." However, this may only be true for concepts that achieve true mass acceptance—down to the "man on the street," as they say.

Chapter 6

1. The history of technical analysis is obscure at best. I have endeavored to be as thorough as possible. Much of the original material was published in newsletters or ancillary documents. Many source documents are simply lost or may have been deliberately destroyed. Much knowledge and many techniques were kept secret, and many of the cognoscenti have passed on, taking their "secrets" with them. Claims are often conflicting, and those who might be able to resolve them frequently have an ax to grind. Any additional citations on bands, envelopes, and related indicators or systems would be greatly appreciated.

2. The typical price is a very old technique. The most commonly used formula is (high + low + close)/3. We would extend it to (open + high + low + close)/4 when the opening price is

available. The use of the typical price to compute the Bollinger Bands is a technique I recommended early on, one that is still quite useful. Using the typical price as a base for Bollinger Bands results in slightly slower, somewhat smoother bands, which may be an advantage in certain applications.

3. Richard Dennis, a famous commodity trader, taught a number of traders his proprietary techniques. Those traders are called Turtles.

4. Hurst, now a recluse, gave a series of seminars in the 1970s in which he expanded greatly upon his work. Much of this material was thought lost until recently when Ed Dobson of Trader's Press in Greenville, South Carolina, contacted Hurst and undertook a project to republish the *CycliTec Services Training Course*. Originally published in 1973, the course consists of three massive binders and a set of audiotapes.

5. *Stock market breadth* refers to market statistics such as advancing and declining issues, the volume of issues up or down on the day, and new 52-week highs and lows. These measures are said to depict how broad the rally is—the theory being, the greater the participation the better.

6. It is this squaring of the deviations from the average that makes Bollinger Bands so adaptive, especially to sudden changes in the price structure.

Chapter 7

1. It turns out that historical volatility and projected or implied volatility are related, and the differences between them contain useful trading information.

2. The population calculation is used for Bollinger Bands, not the estimate calculation for which the divisor changes to $n - 1$. There is no theoretical reason for this. In initial testing the population seemed to work well, and so it was used. The bands would be a bit wider using the estimate calculation.

3. There is another reason, one that is beyond the scope of this book, but which I'll touch upon briefly. Securities prices are not "normally distributed"; they are more variable than one would expect. This is known as having "fat tails." Thus many statistical inferences don't hold. For example, at 30 periods

the bands hold near 89 percent of the data for stocks, rather than the 95.4 percent one would expect. See Chapter 9.

4. An 85 percent containment was initially suggested by Marc Chaikin for Bomar Bands and has proved to be a very useful quantity. So we were pleased to find the containment in these tests running in the same range.

Chapter 8

1. Those of you familiar with technical analysis may recognize George Lane's formula for stochastics as the basis of the above formula. The basic stochastics formula is (last $-$ n-period lowest low)/(n-period highest high $-$ n-period lowest low). Mr. Lane named his indicators %d, %k, etc. So in accordance with his system, and in acknowledgment of the derivation of my approach, I followed his naming scheme and used %b after checking to be sure that Mr. Lane hadn't already used it. George Lane comes from the Midwest, where he barnstormed for many years in a Cessna 210 teaching his trading approach to commodity traders, primarily farmers. He comes from a deeply religious background, and his lectures have the flavor of the revivalist tent. He is not to be missed! He was the first to teach me the idea of three pushes to a high—in a style that I will never forget. It is a concept I have come to appreciate evermore as time has passed. He uses stochastics to diagnose the three-pushes-to-a-high concept; I use Bollinger Bands and volume indicators. I often wonder what indicators he might have come up with had he been more focused on stocks, where volume is concurrently available with price, instead of commodities, where volume is reported a day late and as a single, estimated point.

2. The mathematically inclined will note that using the default settings for Bollinger Bands BandWidth is equal to four times the standard deviation divided by the mean, or four times the coefficient of variation. Again I make no statistical claims on this basis. I only point out the derivations of the calculations we use.

3. Mr. Cahen is also an advocate of the use of three time frames. His approach, which he refers to as his "triptych," consists of

three side-by-side charts featuring increasing time frames from left to right.*

Chapter 9

1. There are two calculations for standard deviation, sample and population. The difference is the final divisor, which is $n - 1$ for the sample and n for the population.
2. GARCH (generalized autoregressive conditional heteroskedasticity) and ARCH (autoregressive conditional heteroskedasticity) are mathematical theories that focus on cyclicity in volatility. For more information see the MathWorks' tutorial chapter on GARCH at http://www.mathworks.com/access/helpdesk/help/toolbox/garch/chap1_tu.shtml. While the whole chapter may be a bit much for most, the first part offers a nice, if terse, overview.

Chapter 10

1. A full discussion of technical patterns is beyond the scope of this book. See Schabacker or Edwards and Magee in the Bibliography.
2. The Lennox System by Sam Kash Kachigan, author of *Statistical Analysis* (see the Bibliography).
3. A fractal displays the same patterns at all levels of magnification. So if a head-and-shoulders pattern were found at the top of the right shoulder of a larger head-and-shoulders pattern the patterns could be said to be fractal. Fractals occur frequently in chaotic systems. A good read on this subject is *Chaos* by James Gleick, New York: Viking, 1987.

Chapter 11

1. For futures contracts, point filters may offer a better view due to the way margin works. When entering into a futures contract, you do not put up the full value of the contract; rather you put up a good-faith deposit, margin, that is the same without regard to price level. So a 1-point move at 20 has the same economic value to a trader as a 1-point move at 100.
2. Macauley's work on the square root rule was most likely done in the early 1930s. But I have been unable to track down the

appropriate issues of the *Annalist* to confirm this. This is the same Fred Macauley who brought you Macauley's modified duration, the standard volatility measurement for bonds. For more on the SRR, see Norm Fosback in *Stock Market Logic* (see the Bibliography).

3. Bollinger Boxes are directly supported by RTR's TechniFilter Plus. To view Bollinger Boxes in TechniFilter, use the form *nnmm%* for the box size, where *nn* is the multiplier and *mm* is the power in the formula 0.*nn* ∗ last^0.*mm*. For simplified Bollinger Boxes, enter 1750 percent for "Boxsize," 3 for "Reversal," and High:Low for "Use" (evaluation method). Our thanks to Clay Burch for his help in this regard (http://www.rtrsoftware.com).

4. The failure of his test is probably due to his use of each stock's volatility as the filter mechanism, which filtered out much of the signal in addition to the noise. When the institutional trading platform www.PatternPower.com was built using the same patterns but Bollinger Boxes instead of a volatility filter, significant results were achieved.

5. Both a capital M and a capital W consist of four strokes connecting five points. There are 32 possible patterns using five points, 2^5.

Chapter 12

1. Mark Douglas defines greed as "fear of not having enough" in his thought-provoking book *The Disciplined Trader* (see the Bibliography). It is interesting to ponder the manifestations of these emotions in that crucible that we call the marketplace; in other words, a market analyst's job is an interesting one by definition.

2. "Down is faster" can be empirically demonstrated. One example: In the spring of 2000 a lightning bear market struck the NASDAQ and the composite fell 37 percent, erasing in 3 weeks gains that had taken 4½ months.

Chapter 13

1. To my mind it is easiest to stick with a series of Ms when analyzing a head-and-shoulders formation, as they are

logically consistent with tops, just as Ws are logically consistent with bottoms.

Chapter 14

1. Indicators such as volume indicators generally come in one of two forms, open or closed. Open-form indicators are usually calculated by keeping a running sum from the point of inception—usually the first data point. Closed-form indicators may also be a sum, but of a given number of periods, 10 or 20 for example. Open-form indicators are usually plotted in the same clip as price to allow direct comparisons, while closed-form indicators are usually plotted in their own clips and are often referred to as oscillators.

2. Elliott's wave pattern can be shown to be a combination of three underlying cycles, where each cycle after the first (shortest) is double the length of the prior cycle. (Once again, the three disparate time frames appear!) This process was demonstrated in my 1986 paper on the subject. Accompanying that paper was a short computer program written in Microsoft BASIC that allowed you to experiment with combining cycles of any lengths and examine the resulting patterns.

Chapter 15

1. The mathematically inclined will quickly note that BandWidth equals four times the standard deviation divided by the mean. The statistically inclined will note that this is four times the coefficient of variation.

2. A more complicated definition of The Squeeze that is taught at our seminars involves Bollinger Bands on volatility itself. First plot the 20-day standard deviation of the close, or typical price. Now plot the 125-day, 1.5 standard deviation width Bollinger Bands of the standard deviation just plotted. A Squeeze is triggered when the 20-day standard deviation tags the lower band.

3. Perhaps the head fake is a corollary of the old "sell on the news" idea. As the new information flows into the market, might traders be taking advantage of it to shift positions,

temporarily distorting market action before the real trend takes hold?

Chapter 16

1. This logic is quite similar to Keltner's Ten-Day Moving Average Rule in its entry logic, but not in its exit logic. Keltner's approach was in the market all the time, long or short. Ours picks occasional trades where the risk-reward is seen as quite favorable.
2. Steve Notis compiled many of these techniques in his Professional Breakout System in the mid-eighties.
3. Parabolics are supported by most technical analysis software today and may be computed by hand. See *New Concepts in Technical Trading Systems* by Welles Wilder for details (see the Bibliography). As published, it was a complete system, but we only use it for exits.

Chapter 17

1. http://www.dictionary.com.
2. For example, Intraday Intensity is designed to reflect the machinations of institutional traders, as they buy and sell positions for their funds. It does so by looking at where we close in a day's range on the assumption that traders will increasingly force price in the direction of their order flow as the day wanes.

Chapter 18

1. Accumulation Distribution relies on the open for its calculation. For many years the *Wall Street Journal* published the opening price along with the rest of the price and volume data each day, but in the early 1970s it dropped the opening price in order to expand its listings. Thus several generations of analysts and traders grew up without access to the open—a shame that was only corrected fairly recently by the advent of broad electronic distribution of stock data.

2. MACD = 12-period exponential average of the last − 26-period exponential average of the last. Signal line = 9-period exponential average of MACD.

3. To calculate a volume-weighted average, multiply each period's price by that period's volume. Then sum the products for the number of periods in the average. Finally, divide the sum by the total volume for the same number of periods. The formula for a 10-day volume-weighted average of the last is 10-day sum of (last ∗ volume)/10-day sum of volume.

Chapter 19

1. The Welles Wilder Parabolic will increment stops in the direction of the trade based on increasing a variable initially set to 0.02 gradually to a terminal value of 0.2. Larger initial values or larger step values will cause the stops to increment more quickly. This will get you out quicker, but is far less forgiving of pullbacks and thus may lead to whipsaws.

Chapter 20

1. We conducted a study of the Arms Index, which confirmed that NYSE trading has a long-term positive bias. The Arms Index depicts the balance between issues traded and the volume in those issues. The formula is (advances/declines)/(up volume/down volume). The Arms Index is neutral at 1, on strong up days it will be less than 1, and on weak days it will be greater than 1. Its long-term average is 0.85, not 1.00 as you might expect. This demonstrates a long-term positive bias to the market that will be reflected in the indicators derived from it, a bias that should be adjusted for.

2. MACD uses exponential averages, which are often expressed as percentages rather than days. To get the percentage value necessary for the calculation when you know the days, use the formula $2/(n+1)$, where n is the number of days.

3. You may lengthen the calculation period to 30 or longer if you are getting too many signals for your taste.

4. 21-day Intraday Intensity or Accumulation Distribution percents are useful here too.

Chapter 21

1. Andrew Cardwell has done a lot of work on this approach to interpreting RSI and is preparing a book on the subject.
2. In 1962, bowling stocks were the Internet stocks of the day and led a speculative rally that collapsed in a lightning-fast bear market. It was believed that bowling would become the great American pastime—that there would be a bowling alley on every block and that everyone would bowl. Automatic pin spotting was the technological key, and vast growth was projected.

Chapter 22

1. One interesting approach is to try using a program like MESA to determine the dominant cycle lengths and set your bars to harmonics of the cycles. For example, if you found an 80-minute cycle, try 20-, 40-, 80-, and 160-minute bars.
2. One way to deal with the volume-distribution problem is by normalizing volume using daily seasonality, but that is beyond the scope of this book.

GLOSSARY

Acceleration: An indicator that measures the rate of change of the rate of change, or the second derivative of price. This measure is most useful for early warnings of changes in trend. See *Velocity* and *Rate of Change*.

Accumulation: The process by which "strong hands" or "those in the know" acquire stock in anticipation of higher prices. This is a core concept for technicians. Many indicators focus on this process, particularly volume indicators. The idea is that before a big move in a stock, there is a period of detectable accumulation during which smart investors accumulate the stock in anticipation of the advance. See *Distribution*.

Accumulation Distribution: A volume indicator based on the relationship of the open to the close of each period. Created by Larry Williams and closely related to the Japanese candlestick concept, hence also known as *Japanese Volume*. The formula is (close − open)/(high − low) ∗ volume. See *Money Flow Index* and *Volume Indicators*.

Advance-Decline Line: An indicator line that is the cumulative sum of the daily number of advancing issues minus declining issues. Its long-term underperformance vis-à-vis the market averages has led many to proclaim it useless. However, as a 21-day sum in conjunction with bands, it is quite an interesting market-timing tool.

Alpha: A mathematical measure of the unique return of a security after the influence of the market has been removed. Equity-Trader.com calculates separate alphas for up and down markets.

Arithmetic Scale: A chart-scaling approach where the distance on the chart is equal for a given point distance regardless of price level. See *Log Scale*.

Arms Index: The Arms Index, created by Richard Arms, is a measure that depicts the balance between the forces of buying and selling in the stock market. The components are advancing and declining issues and up and down volume. At 1.0, those forces are in balance. Above 1.0, the forces of selling predominate. Below 1.0, the buyers are in charge. Due to the long-term upward bias of the market, the average reading for this index runs in the 0.85 area. A very interesting market-timing tool, the Open Arms Index can be created from this index. Also known as the TRIN. The formula is (advances/declines)/(up volume/down volume). See *Open Arms Index*.

Backup: See *Retracement*.

Balanced Fund: Generally, an investment vehicle that contains positions in both bonds and stocks. Some shift the balance as market conditions change. More recently a fund that contains long and short positions.

Bands: Lines drawn around the price structure based on some measure of central tendency. See *Channels* and *Envelopes*.

BandWidth: An indicator derived from Bollinger Bands. The formula is (upper band − lower band)/middle band. See *The Squeeze*.

Bar Chart: A chart with vertical bars representing the trading that occurred during a specific time period, with price on the y axis and time on the x axis. The top of the bar is the high price of the period, the bottom of the bar is the low, the tick to the left is the opening price, and the tick to the right is the closing price.

Base: A period in which a security trades in a relatively narrow range after a decline—usually as a prelude to an advance. It has recently become fashionable to refer to consolidations as *bases*.

Bear Market: An extended period of price decline.

Beta: A mathematical measure of a security's responsiveness to the market. A beta of 1.0 is neutral, 2.0 says the security moves twice as much as the market, and 0.5 means the security moves half as much. EquityTrader calculates separate betas for up and down markets. See *Alpha*.

Black Scholes: The best-known option valuation model. Used to calculate any number of option variables including fair value and implied volatility. A very useful tool, now built into most of the technical analysis software. See a good option book such as *Options as a Strategic Investment* by Lawrence McMillan, New York: New York Institute of Finance, 1986.

Bollinger Bands: Bollinger Bands are bands constructed around a moving average that define in relative terms what is high and what is low. The band width is a multiple of the standard deviation of price. Bollinger Band defaults are a 20-day moving average with 2 standard deviations.

Bollinger Bars: Bars for bar charts where the area between the open and close is shaded red if the close is lower than the open or green if the close is higher. The balance of the bar is blue. Essentially a marriage between a Japanese candlestick and a Western bar.

Bollinger Boxes: A continuous method of specifying the proper box size for point-and-figure charts. Currently supported by RTR's TechniFilter Plus.

Bomar Bands: Trading bands created by Bob Brogan and Marc Chaikin that are spread above and below an average so that 85 percent of the data over the past year is contained.

Bottom: A technical formation of price that marks the low in price for a significant period. V- and W-shaped bottoms are common. The V formation is often called a spike bottom. The W involves two pushes down, the second of which is said to retest the lows established by the first.

Breadth: The number of stocks on an exchange participating in a move. If the number is a large proportion of the total, breadth is said to be good and the move well supported. If the number of issues participating is small, the market is considered thin and sustainability comes into question.

Breakout: A price move that carries prices above a resistance area. Especially a move that ends a trading range. (A breakdown is the same, but carries prices lower rather than higher.)

Bull Market: A sustained period of advancing prices.

Call Option: An option that gives the right, but not the obligation, to the holder to purchase a security at a specific price for a specific period. See *Put Option*.

Candlestick Chart: A Japanese approach to charting in which the relationship of the opening and closing prices governs the color of the body of the "candle" used to depict price action on a chart. These charts can provide substantial insight, especially when the picture is not clear using traditional Western methods. EquityTrader.com uses a form of candlesticks in which the portion of the bar between the open and the close is colored green if the close was higher or red if the close was lower. See *Bollinger Bars*.

Capitalization: The market value of a company—the number of shares outstanding times the last price.

Channels: Areas on a chart where prices trade for an extended period between parallel trend lines. They may be rising, flat, or falling. Channels are most demarked by connecting two or more significant highs or lows and then drawing a parallel line on the opposite side of the formation. Channels may also be drawn around a central line such as a linear-regression line.

ChartCraft: A famous point-and-figure advisory service founded by Abe Cohen.

Close: The final price in a given period. See *Last*.

Closed-End Fund: A mutual fund traded on an exchange. May trade at a premium or discount to its net asset value.

Commissions: The costs of doing a trade exacted by brokers in return for their services.

Confirmation: The state of the market where prices and indicators agree and are therefore said to confirm one another. See *Multicollinearity.*

Congestion Phase: A phase that follows an advance or decline in which prices trade within a narrow range. A trendless period. See *Pivot.*

Consolidation: A pause to refresh after a strong move. Also known as a pivot, because the relative-strength line of a strong stock will flatten or even turn down a bit during a consolidation.

Contrary Opinion: The theory originated by Humphrey Neil that suggests you should go against the crowd. That is, if all are bullish, you should consider the bearish case carefully and vice versa. A very powerful investment approach that works best when extremes are reached.

Convergence: A situation in which trend lines meet or cross—now or in the future. See *Divergence.*

Coppock Curve: A front-weighted averaging technique developed by E. S. C. Coppock, publisher of the classic investment letter *Trendex*. The original Coppock curve used monthly data. Mr. Coppock was the leading exponent of the this-stuff-is-simply-too-good-for-the-likes-of-you approach to investment-letter writing.

Correction: A countermove within the context of a trend that does not break the trend.

Crossover: A signal created when price crosses a threshold, typically a moving average.

Cycle: A regularly occurring event. The four-year presidential cycle is the best example of this in the stock market. There can be volatility cycles too, for example, the 19-day volatility cycle in Treasury bonds.

Deflation: A period in which prices decline. In its more severe forms, deflation is characterized by a contraction in purchasing power as well.

Departure Graph: A graph of the difference of two moving averages, one shorter than the other. Used to measure momentum, departure graphs are the precursors to MACD.

Disinflation: A move toward price stability after an inflation.

Distribution: The process of selling by smart investors, "strong hands," to less astute investors, or "weak hands." It is said to occur at market tops in anticipation of a decline.

Divergence: A state in which trend lines will not meet in the future. For example, if a trend line fit to price is rising and a trend line fit to an indicator is falling, these lines will not cross, no matter how far they are extended into the future. Thus they are said to diverge. If the two lines bear a meaningful relationship to one another, the result is a bearish forecast. See *Convergence*.

Downside: The maximum expected decline in price. Usually considered in a risk-reward evaluation. See *Upside*.

Downtrend: A state in which prices are steadily declining, usually as demarked by a channel. A downtrend is known as a bear market if it is a primary move.

Double Bottom: A bottom formation characterized by an initial low that is successfully retested to complete the formation.

Double Top: A top formation characterized by an initial high followed by a pullback and a try at a subsequent high that fails.

Elliott Wave: A theory developed by R. N. Elliott that all market activity develops in well-ordered patterns consisting of five primary waves and a three-wave correction. These patterns are thought to be nested; any wave can be broken down into a structure similar to its parent. This self-symmetry points toward a fractal quality for the markets which later researchers have corroborated. The Elliott wave and the work of W. D. Gann are the prime examples of the internal-structure approach to the markets. It is thought that these approaches are the keys to great riches. In practice, they explain all that has been extremely eloquently, but little of what will be.

Envelopes: Lines constructed around the price structure without reference to a measure of central tendency such as a moving average that define, on a relative basis, whether prices are high or low. See *Bands* and *Channels*.

EquiVolume: A charting approach in which the x axis is volume instead of time. The approach was developed by Edwin S. Quinn of Investographs and is currently championed by Richard Arms of Arms Index fame. This alternative approach to more traditional chart methods can lead to significant insights. While we do not recommend this as a primary tool, EquiVolume can help clarify patterns that are otherwise opaque.

Exponential Moving Average (EMA): A front-weighted moving average in which each preceding period has diminished importance according to a geometric curve. The EMA is characterized by a very complicated formula that can be elegantly simplified to a computationally simple method, making this a very popular smoothing approach.

Fibonacci: An Italian mathematician known best for discovery of the ratio 1.618 to 1 which may be found many places in nature. It is a derivative of a number series in which each succeeding number is the sum of the prior two. Starting at 1, it goes 1, 1, 2, 3, 5, 8, 13, 21, 34, 55, 89, 144.... For example, $144/89 = 1.618$ and $89/144 = 0.618$. Many believe these ratios to be an aspect of the internal order of the markets.

Filters: Mathematical tools that smooth raw data to aid analysis. My favorites are percentage filters, which eliminate all fluctuations below a specified magnitude. See Arthur Merrill's *Filtered Waves* (see the Bibliography).

Five-Point Patterns: A method of categorizing price patterns using a mathematical filter. There are 32 possible five-point patterns: 16 Ms and 16 Ws.

Fund: Typically a single entity in which several investors have pooled their funds to accomplish a common goal.

Fundamental Analysis: An analytical approach that focuses on the underlying fact set to forecast the future price of a security. For example, an analysis of a company's growth prospects may cause an analyst to believe that a security is too cheap and therefore should be bought. Fundamental analysts believe that their analysis is correct and, if the market price differs, that the market price is incorrect and thus an opportunity exists. Technical analysts believe that the market is correct.

Fundamental Indicators: Valuations of a business or the economy based on the measurement of the cashflow, book value, sales, revenues, etc. Traditionally accounting measures, but often more encompassing these days.

Futures: Contracts that obligate the holder to buy or deliver a commodity at a specific price by a specific date. Usually futures contracts involve a good-faith deposit to ensure performance.

Gann, W. D.: The primary exponent of the internal-order-to-the-markets approach to investing. Gann followers think that there is a secret key to the markets, which, if found, would make the followers wealthy. See *Elliott Wave*.

Gap: A discontinuity in the price structure caused when prices change abruptly; generally caused by new information entering the market while it is closed. Technicians widely regard gaps as important components of the price structure that contain significant information.

Group Power: A daily analytical service available on the web, www.BollingerBands.com, or delivered via e-mail that analyzes the trends in a rational industry-group structure.

Groups: Price indices of groups of companies with similar business characteristics. Rational groups are groups of companies in similar businesses that also have similar trading patterns.

Growth Fund: A mutual fund specializing in growth stocks.

Growth Stock: A stock whose primary determinant of value is the future prospects of the company rather than the present state of the company. Specifically a stock that is expected to grow at a continuingly high rate. A growth-stock company generally pays low or no dividends and thus is hard to analyze using traditional analytical techniques. Occasionally companies arise for which there is no valuation metric; this was the central issue of Internet mania.

Hart, Ed: The late, great commentator on the Financial News Network. Known best for his acerbic commentary and argot such as "compression," "tension on the tape," and the description of the U.S. dollar as a "widows and orphans short."

Head and Shoulders: A technical chart formation consisting of three parts delineated by a neckline and an associated volume pattern. Most often found at tops, it can also be found at bottoms in an inverted form.

Hedge: The combination of two or more securities in such a manner that one offsets certain characteristics (risks) of the other. The object is to combine two securities to make up one trading strategy or position.

Hedge Fund: A specialized type of mutual fund holding simultaneous long and short positions and/or employing leverage. Often hedge funds have international characteristics.

High: The highest price recorded in a given period.

Histogram: A chart with vertical lines representing each data point drawn from a baseline—usually zero—to the data point. A popular technique for plotting indicators.

Hotline: A service that provides updates of investment advice based on the latest market conditions. Originally delivered by telephone, then by fax, and more likely by e-mail these days.

Index: A data series adjusted to some base value, typically 100, as of the starting date or a given reference date. Used to measure stock performance, inflation, or currency values.

Industry Group Analysis: An approach to the market that considers stocks to be members of groups sharing similar business characteristics. Various academic studies have shown industry group and market sectors to be important factors in the returns of portfolios. See *Group Power.*

Industry Groups: Collections of stocks having similar business characteristics. See *Rational Groups.*

Inflation: The trend of decreasing purchasing power over time— typically stated per unit of currency. A 2 percent annual inflation rate means it would take $1.02 to buy next year what can be bought for $1.00 today.

Intermediate Term: A time frame that encompasses market moves of medium importance. Corrections in major bear and bull markets or individual legs within those markets are good examples. May be adjusted according to an investor's time frame.

Intraday Intensity: A volume indicator that depicts the flow of funds for a security based on where it closes in its range. Developed by David Bostian. The formula is $(2 * \text{close} - \text{high} - \text{low})/(\text{high} - \text{low}) * \text{volume}$.

Japanese Volume: See *Accumulation Distribution.*

Last: The most recent price in a given period, whether the period has ended or not. See *Close*.

LEAPS: Long-term options. These are often more sensitive to the underlying assumptions about volatility than to the price of the underlying asset. This often leads to complaints from those who bought LEAPS without understanding how they are priced.

Line Chart: A chart where the data points are connected by a line. Useful where a great deal of data is to be displayed or the data is characterized by a single point.

Liquidity: In essence, the ability to trade. The greater the liquidity, the easier it is to trade. For example, real estate is relatively illiquid, often taking 6 months or more to complete a transaction. On the other hand, high-volume stocks are relatively liquid—a typical transaction can be completed in seconds. The lower the liquidity, the higher the trading costs.

Log Scale: A chart scale that depicts equal-percentage changes rather than point changes for a given distance covered on the *y* axis of a chart—especially useful on long-term charts. See *Arithmetic Scale*.

Long: The state of owning a security—as opposed to short.

Long Term: The major, generally multiyear, trend of markets. For our purposes, six months or longer. For capital gains purposes, 12 months or longer. May be adjusted to suit investor preferences.

Low: The lowest price recorded in a given period.

MACD: See *Moving Average Convergence/Divergence*.

McClellan Oscillator: A breadth oscillator that can be computed for any market that reports the number of advancing and declining issues—usually calculated for the NYSE. See *Breadth*.

Mean: The average value of a data series.

Median: The midpoint of a data series.

Mode: The most common element in a data series.

Momentum: Price change over a given time period, usually expressed in points or as a percent. For example, a very popular and useful momentum measure is the value of the NYSE index today minus the value of that same index 12 days ago. In physics, it is the first derivative. See *Rate of Change*.

Monetary Indicators: Data series such as the Fed funds rate or the growth rate of the money supply that give a clue to the condition of the monetary environment.

Money Flow: Money flow is a much abused term. Three definitions are provided here to try and simplify things. See *Money Flow I, Money Flow II,* and *Money Flow III.*

Money Flow I: Any of a group of indicators designed to measure the ebb and flow of trading in a security by relating price action to volume. See *Accumulation Distribution, Intraday Intensity, Money Flow, On Balance Volume,* and *Positive Volume Index.*

Money Flow II (MFI): A volume-weighted version of Welles Wilder's Relative Strength Index. Very useful.

Money Flow III: Originally developed by Don Worden, also known as tick volume. This is a mathematical assessment of trade-by-trade price and volume action. Current champions include Sam Hale and Lazlo Birinyi.

Moving Average: A measure of the average price (mean) of an item over the previous *n* periods that is recomputed each succeeding period using the most recent data.

Moving Average Convergence/Divergence (MACD): An indicator developed by Gerald Appel that compares the difference between a short average and a longer average. See *Volume-Weighted MACD.*

M-Type Top: A classic chart formation featuring two peaks loosely in the shape of the capital letter M. Often extended to three peaks. By far the most common reversal pattern at tops.

Multicollinearity: A trap in which several indicators seem to confirm each other, but really do not because they are each repeating the same message. A typical example of this is the use of several different momentum indicators.

Mutual Fund: An investment vehicle where many people's funds are pooled together in pursuit of a common goal.

Negative Volume Index (NVI): An indicator based on the theory that important price action occurs on days when volume declines. It seems to us that you have to pick either this or the Positive Volume Index (PVI), but not both. We prefer the PVI. See *Positive Volume Index.*

Net Bulls: A psychological indicator derived from the *Investors Intelligence* survey of investment advisory opinion by subtracting the percentage of bears in the survey from the percentage of bulls, while ignoring those in the correction camp. One of the best ways of assessing market sentiment.

Nonconfirmation: The situation that arises when price action is not echoed by indicator action. Most often a warning of an impending trend reversal.

Normal Distribution: The tendency for things to be distributed in a bell-shaped curve.

Normalized Capitalization: The percentile rank of a company's market value in relation to all other companies. A ranking of 100 is the biggest, and 0 the smallest.

Normalized Indicators: Indicators that have been adjusted to a normalized form using a mathematical transformation such as a stochastic or %b or adjusted by a common factor.

On Balance Volume (OBV): A volume indicator popularized by Joe Granville that looks to the sign of the daily change in its construction. It is a cumulative sum of the sign of the change times volume.

Open: The price of the first trade in a given period.

Open Arms Index: This is a version of the Arms Index that is created from averages of the components rather than the average of the index itself. The 10-day Open Arms Index is a useful market-timing tool that gives buy signals in the 1.10 to 1.20 area. The same result can be obtained by averaging the logs of the one-day Arms Index readings and then taking the antilog. See *Arms Index.*

Open-End Fund: A mutual fund that can be bought from or sold to the fund company at its net asset value.

Options: Financial contracts that confer the right but not the obligation to buy or sell a given security or index for a specified amount of time. Calls confer the right to buy and puts the right to sell.

Oscillator: An indicator that oscillates above and below a given value—usually 0—or one that is bounded between two values and is thus said to oscillate. As opposed to open-ended indicators that may rise and fall as they please. Often a given indicator may come in both forms.

Overbought: Currently the state of a price having risen too far, too fast. In former times, the word had more climactic implications.

Oversold: The opposite of overbought.

Pairs: The mating of securities having opposing qualities—often a hedge fund strategy.

%b: An indicator derived from the position of the last data point in relation to Bollinger Bands. %b equals 1.0 at the upper band, .5 at the middle band, and 0 at the lower band. The formula is (last − lower Bollinger Band)/(upper Bollinger Band − lower Bollinger Band).

Persistence: The percentage of days in the last n days in which an indicator was positive. Typically used with Intraday Intensity where persistence is the percentage of days in the past six months for which the money flow measure was positive.

Pivot: A consolidation by a strong stock in which its relative-strength line goes flat, followed by a resumption of the trend. In addition, a reaction signal generated after a PowerShift.

Point and Figure: A type of chart that records only price action without reference to time. See *Bollinger Boxes*.

Point-and-Figure Swing: The direction of the current move as depicted by point-and-figure rules. The direction of the last point-and-figure reversal.

Positive Volume Index (PVI): An indicator based on the theory that days when the volume increases are important. It is an accumulation of price change on days when volume expands versus the prior day. See *Negative Volume Index*.

PowerShift: A technical signal that arises from an oversold or overbought condition when sufficient strength or weakness to break the trend is detected. (See www.EquityTrader.com.)

Price Filters: Mathematical tools designed to clarify patterns by reducing short-term noise.

Psychological or Sentiment Indicators: Data pertaining to the attitudes and feelings of market participants. Surveys regarding bullish or bearish sentiment or counts of bullish and bearish bets in the options market are typical examples. The most famous are the *Investors Intelligence* poll of investment advisers and the put-call ratio. These indicators are to be treated in a contrarian manner at the extremes.

Pullback: Price movement against the primary trend that does not interrupt that trend.

Put-Call Ratio: Attributed to Marty Zweig, a sentiment indicator derived from options trading.

Put Option: An option that confers the right, but not the obligation, to sell a security at a given price for a given time. See *Call Option*.

Pyramid: A hierarchical stock market structure consisting of four layers: Stocks are at the lowest level, industry groups are next, market sectors are next, and the markets at the peak. Currently Group Power contains 3700 stocks organized into 150 groups, 13 sectors, and 1 market in its pyramid.

Rate of Change: Price change over a given period usually expressed as a percentage. For example, the 12-day rate of change of the NYSE Composite is thought to be a good overbought-oversold indicator for the market. This is a component of our Market Model. See *Momentum*.

Rational Analysis: The juncture of the sets of technical analysis and fundamental analysis.

Rational Groups: Collections of stocks that have common business characteristics and similar trading patterns; the basis of Group Power.

Reaction: See *Correction*.

Relative Strength: Relative strength is the relationship of an item to an index or to a basket of items. At its simplest, the relative-strength line is the price of a stock divided by the price of the S&P 500. A bit more complex would be a relative-strength ranking where the price action of an item over a given period is compared with the price action of the other items in the universe over the same period.

Relative Strength Index (RSI): Created by Welles Wilder. An indicator that compares the action of a security on the days on which it rose with the action of the same security on the days on which it fell. In effect, a ratio of a security's strength to its weakness. See *Money Flow II*.

Resistance Area: An area on a chart above current prices where identifiable trading has occurred before. It is thought that investors who bought at those higher prices will become sellers when those prices are reached again, thus halting an advance.

Retracement: A minor move against the main trend that "retraces" some of the prior move. The giveback of a portion of a primary move. Key retracement levels are considered to be one-third, one-half, and two-thirds of the prior move. Many people use Fibonacci numbers to calculate retracement targets.

Risk-Adjusted Return: The annualized return of a security divided by negative beta if negative beta is greater than 1. Essentially, annualized return penalized by downside volatility.

Sectors: Aggregations of industry groups with common economic themes. Basic materials and technology are good examples of sectors.

Securities: Investments that can be bought and sold as small portions of the whole—a share of stock in a company or a bond, for example.

Sell on the News: The idea that once good news, especially heavily anticipated good news, is out, it is best to sell, as profit taking is bound to occur. A variation is the concept that once the news is out, there is little to propel the stock higher. The trading-floor cynic says, "Buy on the rumor. Sell on the news."

Setback: A temporary decline, as in the decline often seen after good news.

Setup: A combination of factors that leads to a trade with a high probability of success. For example, a band tag accompanied by a nonconfirmation from an indicator or a W bottom.

Short: The state of being short a security. The act of selling before buying, thus a bet on prices falling. The trading-floor cynic says, "He who sells what isn' hisn' must buy it back or go to pris'n."

Short Covering: The closing side of a short transaction. Often said to help prices move higher in a hurry, as short sellers desperate to close their positions pay any price for the privilege of doing so.

Short Interest: The amount of outstanding short sales in shares.

Short Term: A time frame determined by the price swings within an intermediate-term move. A correction to an intermediate-term uptrend would be a short-term downtrend. For our purposes, 1 to 10 days. For tax purposes, less than 12 months.

Sideline Bar & Grill: A comfortable place from which one can observe the action without being involved. For example, cash during a period of transition or volatility. A favorite haunt of the trading-floor cynic.

Simple Moving Average: The most common type of moving average. Each period receives equal weighting. Along with the trend line, the most basic of technical tools.

Slippage: The difference between the price you wanted and the price you got. A major drag on performance. See *Transaction Costs*.

Spike Top: A top that stands alone, characterized by a sharp advance and a sudden, sharp decline without any warning.

Square Root Rule (SRR): A rule attributed to Fred Macauley that suggests that for a given move in the market, prices of individual stocks will move by an amount such that their square roots will change by equal amounts. This implies that lower-priced stocks will be more volatile that high-priced issues.

Standard Deviation: A mathematical measure of volatility that measures deviations from an average, σ. The basis of the Bollinger Bands.

Stochastic: A measure of where we are in percentage terms in the previous n-day trading range. A 10-day stochastic of 70 would say we are 70 percent of the way from the lowest low to the highest high of the previous 10 days' trading.

Stock: A share in the ownership of a company that can be traded on a securities exchange. The trading-floor cynic notes that a stock is not to be confused with the company itself.

Stubbornness (Stupidity): The concept of selling only when you can get out whole. As contrasted to being smart and saving as much capital as you can by exiting a losing trade and looking for a more profitable opportunity.

Support: An area where declines halt and are reversed. Support is often associated with perceived value. The opposite of resistance.

Technical Analysis: An analytical approach based on the belief that price reflects all that is knowable about a security at any given time. Therefore, the price structure itself is the best source of data for forecasting future prices.

Technical Indicators: Usually mathematical constructs of price, volume, or other factors that serve to illuminate decision making. Typically focused on the balance between supply and demand.

The Squeeze: A period of reduced volatility that leads to a period of increased volatility. A six-month low in volatility serves as a Squeeze alert.

Tick Volume: The number of price changes or price postings in a day or any given period.

Time Frame: Time frames are centered on the time horizons you actually trade, which we refer to as the intermediate-term time frame. For us, it is approximately 20 days. The intermediate time frame is bracketed by two other time frames, short term and long term. The short-term time frame is the one in which you execute trades. The long-term time frame provides the background for your market operations. Old-time technicians thought of short term as the action on day charts, intermediate term as the action on weekly charts, and long term as the action on monthly charts. Today a trader using five-minute bar charts might think of intermediate term as a half hour. Time frames are entirely dependent on your reference. Whatever the reference, you should always pay attention to the time frames that bracket your intermediate-term plan.

Top: An area on a price chart that leads to an important decline. Usually the highest point achieved in recent times.

Trading Bands: Intervals constructed around the price structure that provide a relative framework for price analysis and/or the interpretation of indicators.

Trading-Floor Cynic: A wise, but rather cynical, conduit of market fact, fiction, intelligence, lore, and rumor.

Trading Range: A price range in which trading has been confined for an extended period. Generally sideways in character, but a given range may rise or fall over time. Trading ranges can be consolidation patterns leading to a continuation of the prior move. They can also be reversal areas, in which case they are identified as bottoms or tops. The techniques an analyst employs within a trading range are quite different from those employed in a trending market. For example, oscillators such as RSI are useful in identifying reversals at the top or bottom of a trading range, but are less applicable when the market is trending. In trending markets, trend-following approaches such as moving averages or regression channels are more useful.

Transaction Costs: The cost of doing a trade—primarily slippage and commissions.

Trap: A series of circumstances and/or price movements that cause one to take the wrong position. An example of a bull trap is a breakout to the upside that convinces you prices are going higher, but is followed by a sharp decline. A bear trap is the inverse, a sag to a new low followed by a strong advance.

Trend: The overall direction of the item being considered.

Trend Line: A line drawn on a chart to help determine the trend of the item being charted. Typically connecting important highs or lows.

Triangle: A congestion pattern during which volatility steadily diminishes.

TRIN: See *Arms Index*.

Typical Price: A measure of the average price recorded during a given period. Often a better characterization than the close. The formula is (high + low + close)/3 or (open + high + low + close)/4.

Upside: The maximum expected advance in price over a given horizon, usually considered in a risk-reward evaluation. See *Downside*.

Uptrend: A period of steadily higher prices.

Velocity: The rate of change of price. Used most often to recognize a change in trend prior to a reversal formation coming into being. See *Rate of Change*.

VIX: The Chicago Board of Options Volatility Index. Useful for detecting panic lows.

Volatility: The tendency for prices to vary. There are many measures of volatility. Standard deviation is one of the more popular.

Volatility-Breakout Systems: Trading systems designed to trigger when volatility exceeds a certain level. The most interesting of these require that volatility be low to start with.

Volume: The number of transactions or the quantity of items traded in a given period.

Volume Indicators: Technical indicators designed to get to the heart of the supply-demand equation by integrating volume.

Volume-Price Trend: A variation on On Balance Volume developed by David Markstein that uses percent change in the calculation.

Volume-Weighted MACD: A version of MACD developed by Buff Dormeier that uses volume-weighted averages rather than exponential averages.

Warrants: Essentially, long-term options.

Washout: A sell-off that leads to a total lack of interest, an abandoning of hope. Often the first stage of a base-building process that leads to a rally.

W Bottom: The most typical bottom formation. An initial low point followed by a rally and a retest of the low. Generally in the shape of a capital W.

Wedge: A consolidation pattern typically characterized by rising bottoms or declining tops.

Weighted Moving Average: A moving average in which the weights assigned to each day in the calculation are different. A typical version is the front-weighted moving average in which the most recent periods figure more heavily in the calculation than prior periods.

Whipsaw: A sell followed immediately by a buy, or vice versa. Often expensive due to transaction costs.

Wyckoff, Richard D.: A technical analyst operating in the early part of the twentieth century whose work stands out even after all these years.

Yield Curve: A depiction of interest rate levels versus maturities in graphic form with short-term rates at the left and long-term rates at the right. Generally, Treasury debt is the subject. In normal times, short-term rates are lower than long-term rates. Thus, the curve rises from left to right and is said to be positively sloped.

Zigzag: An alternating pattern of advances followed by declines typically defined by some minimum price swing.

BIBLIOGRAPHY

Bollinger, John, "Volume Indicators," Bollinger Capital, 2000.

Burke, Michael, *The All New Guide to the Three-Point Reversal Method of Point & Figure Construction and Formulas*, ChartCraft, New Rochelle, N.Y., 1990.

Cahen, Philippe, "Analyse Technique Dynamique," *Economica*, 1999.

Crane, Burton, *The Sophisticated Investor*, Simon and Schuster, New York, 1959.

deVilliers, Victor, *The Point and Figure Method of Anticipating Common Stock Price Movements*, 1933, reprinted Windsor Books, New York.

Douglas, Mark, *The Disciplined Trader*, New York Institute of Finance, New York, 1990.

Drew, Garfield A., *New Methods for Profit in the Stock Market*, 1955, reprinted by Fraser Publishing, Burlington, Vt.

Edwards, Robert D., and John Magee, *Technical Analysis of Stock Trends*, 5th ed., John Magee, Inc., Boston, Mass., 1966.

The Encyclopedia of Stock Market Techniques, Investors Intelligence, New Rochelle, N.Y., 1985.

Fosback, Norman G., *Stock Market Logic*, The Institute for Econometric Research, Fort Lauderdale, Fla., 1990.

Holmes, Oliver Wendell, *The Common Law*, 1881, reprinted by Dover Publications, Boston, Mass., 1991.

Hurst, J. M., *The Profit Magic of Stock Transaction Timing*, 1970, reprinted by Traders Press, Greenville, S.C.

Kachigan, Sam Kash, *Statistical Analysis*, Radius Press, New York, 1982.

Keltner, Chester W., *How to Make Money in Commodities*, The Keltner Statistical Service, Kansas City, Mo., 1960.

Levy, Robert, "The Predictive Significance of Five-Point Chart Patterns," *The Journal of Business*, July 1971.

Mandlebrot, Benoit B., *Fractal Geometry of Nature*, Freeman, 1988.

Merrill, Arthur A., *Behavior of Prices on Wall Street*, Analysis Press, Chappaqua, N.Y., 1984.

————, *Filtered Waves, Basic Theory*, 3rd ed., Analysis Press, Chappaqua, N.Y., 1977.

————, *M & W Wave Patterns*, 3rd ed., Analysis Press, Chappaqua, N.Y., 1983.

Schabacker, Richard W., *Technical Analysis and Stock Market Profits*, 1932, reprinted by Pitman, London, England, 1997.

Schmidt, W. C., *Peerless Stock Market Timing*, San Diego, Calif., 1982.

Shimizu, Seiki, *The Japanese Book of Charts*, Tokyo Futures Trading Publishing, Tokyo, 1986.

Stutely, Richard, *The Economist Number Guide*, John Wiley & Sons, New York, 1998.

Weiss, Geraldine, and Janet Lowe, *Dividends Don't Lie*, Longman, Chicago, Ill., 1989.

Wheelan, Alexander H., *Study Helps in Point and Figure Technique*, Morgan, Rogers, and Roberts, 1947, reprinted by Fraser Publishing, Burlington, Vt., 1989.

White, Michael, and John Gribbin, *Einstein: A Life in Science*, Dutton Books, New York, 1994.

Wilder, J. Welles Jr., *New Concepts in Technical Trading Systems*, Trend Research, Greensboro, S.C., 1978.

Yates, James, *The Options Strategy Spectrum*, Dow Jones–Irwin, Homewood, Ill., 1987.

INDEX

ABOUT THE AUTHOR

John Bollinger is president and founder of Bollinger Capital Management, an investment management company that provides technically driven money management services to individuals, corporations, trusts, and retirement plans. Bollinger Capital Management also develops and provides proprietary research for institutions and individuals. Bollinger publishes *Capital Growth Letter* and provides weekly commentary and analysis on CNBC, and he was for years the chief market analyst on Financial News Network. He is both a frequent contributor as well as a featured expert for publications including *The Wall Street Journal*, *Investor's Business Daily*, *Barron's*, *Technical Analysis of Stocks and Commodities*, *The New York Times*, *Los Angeles Times*, and *USA Today*.

15 BASIC RULES

1. Bollinger Bands provide a relative definition of high and low.
2. That relative definition can be used to compare price action and indicator action to arrive at rigorous buy and sell decisions.
3. Appropriate indicators can be derived from momentum, volume, sentiment, open interest, intermarket data, etc.
4. Volatility and trend already have been deployed in the construction of Bollinger Bands, so their use for confirmation of price action is not recommended.
5. The indicators used for confirmation should not be directly related to one another. Two indicators from the same category do not increase confirmation. Avoid collinearity.
6. Bollinger Bands can be used to clarify pure price patterns such as M-type tops and W-type bottoms, momentum shifts, etc.
7. Price can, and does, walk up the upper Bollinger Band and down the lower Bollinger Band.
8. Closes outside the Bollinger Bands can be continuation signals, not reversal signals—as is demonstrated by the use of Bollinger Bands in some very successful volatility-breakout systems.
9. The default parameter of 20 periods for calculating the moving average and standard deviation and the default parameter of 2 standard deviations for the BandWidth are just that, defaults. The actual parameters needed for any given market or task may be different.
10. The average deployed should not be the best one for crossover signals. Rather, it should be descriptive of the intermediate-term trend.
11. If the average is lengthened, the number of standard deviations needs to be increased simultaneously—from 2 at 20 periods to 2.1 at 50 periods. Likewise, if the average is shortened, the number of standard deviations should be reduced—from 2 at 20 periods to 1.9 at 10 periods.
12. Bollinger Bands are based upon a simple moving average. This is because a simple moving average is used in the standard deviation calculation and we wish to be logically consistent.
13. Be careful about making statistical assumptions based on the use of the standard deviation calculation in the construction of the bands. The sample size in most deployments of Bollinger Bands is too small for statistical significance, and the distributions involved are rarely normal.
14. Indicators can be normalized with %b, eliminating fixed thresholds in the process.
15. Finally, tags of the bands are just that—tags, not signals. A tag of the upper Bollinger Band is *not* in and of itself a sell signal. A tag of the lower Bollinger Band is *not* in and of itself a buy signal.

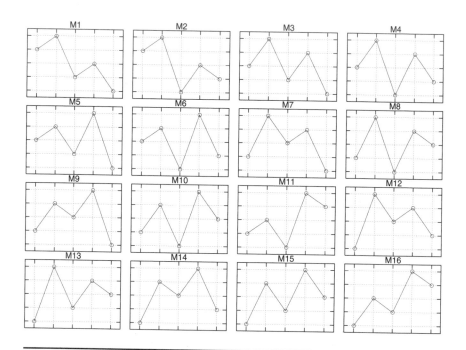

Technical Patterns | Merrill's Patterns

Technical Patterns	Merrill's Patterns
Uptrends (higher highs):	M15, M16, W14, W16
Downtrends (lower lows):	M1, M3, W1, W2
Head and shoulders:	W6, W7, W9, W11, W13, W15
Inverted head and shoulders:	M2, M4, M6, M8, M10, M11
Triangle (narrowing):	M13, W4
Megaphone (broadening):	M5, W12

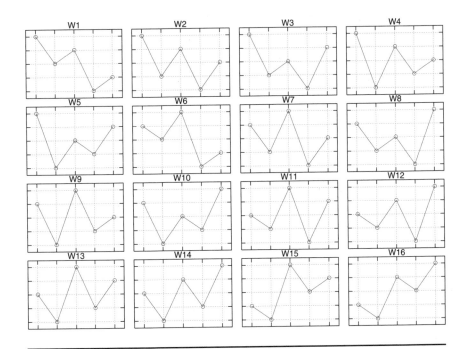

Technical Patterns	Merrill's Patterns
Uptrends (higher highs):	M15, M16, W14, W16
Downtrends (lower lows):	M1, M3, W1, W2
Head and shoulders:	W6, W7, W9, W11, W13, W15
Inverted head and shoulders:	M2, M4, M6, M8, M10, M11
Triangle (narrowing):	M13, W4
Megaphone (broadening):	M5, W12

BOLLINGER BAND FORMULAS

20-Day Moving Average

$$\bar{c} = \sum\nolimits_1^{20} c_i / 20$$

20-Day Standard Deviation

$$s = \sqrt{\frac{\sum_1^{20}(c_i - \bar{c})^2}{20}}$$

Upper Bollinger Band

$$\bar{c} + 2 * s$$

Middle Bollinger Band

$$\bar{c}$$

Lower Bollinger Band

$$\bar{c} - 2 * s$$

Bollinger Band Parameters

Length	Width
10	1.9
20	2.0
50	2.1

%b

$$\frac{(\text{last} - \text{lower band})}{(\text{upper band} - \text{lower band})}$$

BandWidth

$$\frac{(\text{upper band} - \text{lower band})}{\text{middle band}}$$

VOLUME INDICATOR FORMULAS

50-Day Volume Moving Average

$$\bar{v} = \sum\nolimits_1^{50} v_i / 50$$

Normalized Volume

$$v / \bar{v} * 100$$

Intraday Intensity

$$\sum\nolimits_1^{\infty} ((2c - h - l)/(h - l) * v)$$

Accumulation Distribution

$$\sum\nolimits_1^{\infty} ((c - o)/(h - l) * v)$$

Money Flow Index

$$t = (h + l + c)/3$$

$$100 - \left(\frac{100}{\left(1 + \sum_1^n (t > t_{-1} * v) \middle/ \sum_1^n (t < t_{-1} * v)\right)} \right)$$

Where the default for n is 14.

Volume-Weighted MACD

$$\sum_1^n c_i * v_i \middle/ \sum_1^n v_i - \sum_1^m c_i * v_i \middle/ \sum_1^m v_i$$

Where $n =$ periods in the short-term average and $m =$ periods in the long-term average.

20-Day OBV Oscillator

$$\sum_1^{20} (((c > c_{-1}) - (c < c_{-1})) * v)$$

21-Day Normalized II Oscillator

$$\sum_1^{21} [(2c - h - l)/(h - l) * v] \middle/ \sum_1^{21} v_i * 100$$

Key:
$c =$ close
$h =$ high
$l =$ low
$o =$ open
$v =$ volume
The subscript -1 refers to the prior day.